"Sam Allberry flushes out the several hidden, barely conscious assumptions about singleness and celibacy that control our attitudes toward single living. Once he makes these assumptions visible, he uses the Bible to dismantle them and show us a better way. It would be a great mistake, however, if we were to think this is a book only for singles. If Sam is right—and he is—the entire church must understand the biblical teaching on this subject. The local congregation must be not merely a loose network of families but a close-knit family itself, consisting of both married couples and singles, all living together as brothers and sisters. This volume will show us how to do that."

Timothy J. Keller, Pastor Emeritus, Redeemer Presbyterian Church, New York City

"*7 Myths about Singleness* offers a refreshing, biblical perspective on an oft-neglected topic. Allberry writes to remove the stigma from the idea of singleness and to help Christians think biblically about the callings of singles within the body of Christ. This timely resource will benefit the church for years to come."

Russell D. Moore, President, The Ethics & Religious Liberty Commission of the Southern Baptist Convention

"*7 Myths about Singleness* makes the glory of Jesus, a single man, more obvious in ways helpful to us all. Sam Allberry opens our eyes to how we can better understand ourselves and one another, how we can better steward our married or single lives, and especially how we can stop chasing the myths that break our hearts. He does this by showing us more of Jesus where it can be hard to find him—in the real lives we are living right now. So this married man was turning these pages thinking, "*I* need this. *I* am helped by this!" I think you too will be helped."

Ray Ortlund, Lead Pastor, Immanuel Church, Nashville, Tennessee

"Far too often, the church regards single Christians as people who need to be fixed or fixed up. Sam Allberry provides a pastoral guide to correct this and help the church live like the family of God. I am grateful to God for Sam Allberry and for this new book!"

Rosaria Butterfield, Former Professor of English, Syracuse University; author, *The Gospel Comes with a House Key*

"Sam Allberry, in true form, doesn't waste a single word in *7 Myths about Singleness*. His tone, structure, humor, and biblical undergirding make this book one of the best on the subject in recent years. Not only has Allberry thought hard about the subject of singleness; he has lived it and continues to glorify Christ in it. Too often, books on singleness still make marriage—or at least becoming marriageable—the point. There is none of that in here. Instead he dissembles the lies in which the unmarried can find themselves trapped, showing the abundant life Christ offers to every single person. People often ask me for the best book on singleness, and I'm grateful to have finally found one."

Lore Ferguson Wilbert, author, *Handle with Care: Why Jesus Came to Touch and How We Should Too*

*7 Myths
about
Singleness*

7 Myths about Singleness

Sam Allberry

CROSSWAY®

WHEATON, ILLINOIS

Published in association with the literary agency of Wolgemuth & Associates, Inc.

Cover design: Micah Lanier

First printing 2019

Printed in the United States of America

Trade paperback ISBN: 978-1-4335-6152-8
ePub ISBN: 978-1-4335-6155-9
PDF ISBN: 978-1-4335-6153-5
Mobipocket ISBN: 978-1-4335-6154-2

Library of Congress Cataloging-in-Publication Data

Names: Allberry, Sam, author.
Title: 7 myths about singleness / Sam Allberry.
Other titles: Seven myths about singleness
Description: Wheaton : Crossway, 2019. | Includes bibliographical references and index.
Identifiers: LCCN 2018026102 (print) | LCCN 2018034459 (ebook) | ISBN 9781433561535 (pdf) | ISBN 9781433561542 (mobi) | ISBN 9781433561559 (epub) | ISBN 9781433561528 (tp)
Subjects: LCSH: Single people—Religious life.
Classification: LCC BV4596.S5 (ebook) | LCC BV4596.S5 A425 2018 (print) | DDC 261.8/358153—dc23
LC record available at https://lccn.loc.gov/2018026102

Crossway is a publishing ministry of Good News Publishers.

BP		29	28	27	26	25	24	23	22	21	20	19
15	14	13	12	11	10	9	8	7	6	5	4	3	2	1

For
Brian and Leslie Roe and Daniel and Sarah Roe,
Dan and April DeWitt,
Tim and Kathy Keller,
Ray and Jani Ortlund,
with thanks for giving me a key, making me a part of
your family, and giving me a home away from home

Contents

Introduction

It turns out there are many things we don't know quite as well as we think we do.

One of the most popular comedy shows in the United Kingdom is *QI* (short for "Quite Interesting"). Each week the panelists are presented with interesting and little-known facts to discuss. Part of the show is dedicated to "general ignorance," things commonly assumed to be facts that are actually untrue. You do not, it turns out, have two nostrils, but four (two of them you can't see). Mount Everest, it turns out, is not the tallest in the world (it is the highest, but not the tallest). King Henry VIII did not, it turns out, have six wives (it's complicated). The earth, it turns out, does not have just one moon (there are all sorts of other nonman-made things floating around us that technically count as moons).[1] And so it goes on. Oftentimes, it seems, we know a good deal less than we think.

This is true not just of mountains, moons, kings, and nostrils but of singleness as well. Much of what we commonly assume to be the case with singleness is either flat-out untrue or, at the very least, really shouldn't be true. Almost all these things are negatives about singleness, as we shall see. In much of our thinking, singleness, if not downright *bad*, is certainly not seen as good. One writer has noted the difference between

Christian books on marriage and those on singleness.[2] In the books on marriage, marriage is assumed to be a great thing, and all that remains is to understand it better and perhaps be aware of one or two potential pitfalls that might arise. But books on singleness typically have a different starting point. Singleness is assumed to be pretty much awful; the point of the books is, therefore, to see if we might be able to eke out something just about tolerable from it.

Even the way we describe singleness reflects this. It is almost always defined in the negative, as the absence of something. It's the state of not being married. It is the absence of a significant other. This defining by negation reinforces the idea that there is nothing intrinsically good about singleness; it is merely the situation of lacking what is intrinsically good in marriage.

I often see this when people are having some sort of introductory conversation. When someone asks, "Are you married?" or, "Do you have family?" and we answer in the affirmative, the person asking is delighted, and it sparks a fresh round of discussion about how you and your spouse met or the age of your children. But when answered in the negative, people often don't quite know what to do with it, and the conversation grinds to a halt. Marriage is a conversational intersection, with all sorts of interesting avenues of discussion. Singleness is more of a conversational cul-de-sac, requiring an awkward maneuver to exit.

It is worth pointing out what we mean by "singleness," as this will have a significant bearing on our discussion. From the point of view of Christianity, to be single means being both unmarried and committed (for as long as we remain unmarried) to sexual abstinence. The Bible is clear that sex outside of marriage is sinful, something that is underlined in the teaching of Jesus. To be single is to refrain from any sexual behavior. If you're single long term, as a Christian that means being sexually abstinent long term.

This is very different from the predominantly secular culture around us, which holds that to be single involves the former (being unmarried) but not the latter (sexual abstinence). And since marriage is often seen as a constraint in many ways, being single in a secular context can be thought of as a positive boon. You have the freedom to find sexual fulfillment without any of the commitments that come with marriage. You are free to play the field in whichever way you think might make you happy. A prominent British journalist and broadcaster, Mariella Frostrup, described singleness as "solvency, great sex, and a guilt-free life."[3]

So singleness for the Christian can look very different from singleness for someone who is not. It is little wonder, then, that so many think of Christian notions of celibacy and chasteness as unappealing. I just realized as I typed those two words, "celibacy" and "chasteness," just how old-fashioned they seem. They sound more like they'd belong in *Downton Abbey* than in contemporary life. I suspect there's a very simple reason for that: there are no equivalent contemporary notions today, so we can only borrow language from previous generations to describe it. Celibacy is, frankly, weird for most people today. Harmful, even. So with this cultural backdrop, it is no surprise to find so many within the church thinking along similar lines.

This is where "general ignorance" quickly kicks in. Henry VIII didn't actually have six wives. And singleness isn't actually a bad thing. In the Bible it's good. It's even described as a blessing. In and of itself it's a wonderful gift from God that should be affirmed and celebrated. Read on, and I hope you'll find out why.

Most of what we think we know is actually untrue. And the point of this book is that the goodness of singleness is something the whole church needs to know. It's obvious that singles need to be clear about it, but so too does everybody else. The Bible's teaching on singleness is given to all of God's people.

The most lengthy and thorough discussion of singleness comes in 1 Corinthians 7, and at first glance it seems to contradict the point I've just made. As Paul takes us through issues of marriage and singleness he turns to different sections of the readership and addresses them directly: "To the unmarried and the widows I say . . ." (v. 8); "To the married I give this charge . . ." (v. 10); "To the rest I say . . ." (v. 12). But here's the thing: even as Paul addresses each of these groups specifically, he wants and expects the whole church to be listening in. I am not a widow (and can never be one). But the Scriptures addressed to them are still given to me. I must not skip over them. Similarly, though I am not a parent, passages directed to parents are still God's word to me. The same is the case with Scriptures about singleness, even when directed to singles. God's word to singles about singleness is something you need to know about, whatever your stage of life or marital status. There are two reasons for this.

First, most of us who are married will one day be single again. We don't like to dwell on this reality if we're married. But think about it. It is rare for a married couple to die at the same time. As I write this, it is twenty-four years pretty much to the day since my grandmother died. Our family was devastated, and no one more so than her husband, my grandfather "Pop." None of us was sure how he would cope, even with a large and supportive family who cherish him. Yet he has had to experience singleness for whole decades since she died. Pop is not far from spending more of his life unmarried than married, which is something, given that they were married for over fifty years (he is only a few months shy of turning one hundred).

Bereavement will return many who are married now to singleness again. It is sobering and sad to think about, but also necessary. Add to that the number of marriages that will end in divorce, and the proportion of those who will become single for a second time rises even higher. A ring on our finger now is no sure sign that we will not be single in the future. Better to think carefully and biblically about singleness now rather than later.

Second, singleness directly affects all of us. The Bible repeatedly speaks of the local church as a body, which means that we aren't free to come and go from it without obligation. No, Paul tells us, "For just as each of us has one body with many members, and these members do not all have the same function, so in Christ we, though many, form one body, and each member belongs to all the others" (Rom. 12:4–5 NIV). We're a body. We belong to one another. What happens to part of us therefore affects all. If some struggle, it hurts us all. We're invested in one another, and therefore I need to know what the Christian life is like for you in your situation, and you need to know what it's like for me in mine.

This applies far more widely than merely to issues of marriage and singleness. But it shows me that as a single person, I have a stake in the health of the marriages in my church family. And those who are married have a stake in the health of my singleness. It's part of what belonging to one another involves. And when we think of the proportion of our local church that might be single, it makes it all the more urgent that we're all on the same page, talking about the same thing, and heading in the same direction. It is in the interests of all of us, the whole church, single and married, to understand the positive vision the Bible gives us of singleness.

But that'll involve overturning some common misconceptions.

1

Singleness Is Too Hard

In wider culture, singleness (as we have already noted) is not a problem in and of itself. But *celibacy* is. It is fine not to have married. It can even be a good thing—you are footloose and fancy-free. (Though I confess I've no idea what either of those terms actually means.) But to be without sexual or romantic intimacy is another matter.

Two recent movies highlight this.[1] Take the Steve Carell comedy *The 40-Year-Old Virgin*. The whole premise behind it is that to be a virgin at forty years old is utterly laughable. People are horrified when they find out. Some treat him like a child. After all, he's not properly grown up yet. And, of course, the happy ending to the movie is that he finally does lose his virginity. Although the impact on him is overblown, the point is real: he's now entered into one of the key things life is about.

Another example is the movie *Forty Days and Forty Nights*. The tagline says it all: "One man is about to do the unthinkable. No sex. Whatsoever. For forty days and forty nights." Think about that for a moment. Forty days and forty nights is neither an arbitrary length of time nor an arbitrary way of describing it. In the Gospel accounts Jesus was in the wilderness without food for "forty days and forty nights" (Matt. 4:2). Christians observing Lent typically give something up for the same period of time. Forty days and forty nights has become the standard unit for those who want to be serious about depriving themselves of something. We're willing to go this long without chocolate or carbs or social media or TV. But to go this long without sex? *Unthinkable.* I've just calculated that I've done the equivalent length of time well over two hundred times. Once is unthinkable. Two hundred plus? Well, I am *way* off the charts. I heard someone describe long-term celibates like me as being like unicorns: you've heard of them, but you never think you're going to actually meet one.

Behind the comedy of such movies lies a serious belief, one that is widespread in the Western world today: without sex you can't really experience what it means to be truly human. According to this thinking, our sense of personhood is directly attached to our sex life. To ignore this side of us, to deliberately not express and fulfill it, is to actually do harm to ourselves. It is a fundamental aspect of our humanity, and repressing it is not healthy. Those who are long-term single are not just quaint and old-fashioned; we might actually be deluded. Something is very wrong with us.

Choosing to live this way is questionable enough, but there is a unique distaste for those who might, in the name of religion, require it of anybody else. Calling others to live sexually abstinent outside of marriage is now regarded as unnecessary and cruel. Those wanting to uphold the Bible's teaching on sexual ethics are criticized for "enforcing celibacy" on others and, by doing so, causing considerable damage.

All this means we need to be crystal clear about what the Bible really says about these things.

Jesus on Sex and Marriage

One of the prevailing myths today is that Jesus was tolerant when it comes to sexual ethics. Sure, people tend to think, the Old Testament had some strict things to say about marriage and sexuality, and Paul was evidently having the theological equivalent of a bad-hair day when he was writing some of his letters, but Jesus was much more relaxed about these things and didn't seem to have any of the hang-ups that his followers today are accused of having.

But it is wrong to suggest Jesus had nothing challenging to say about sex. In fact, he takes the broad Old Testament sexual ethic and intensifies it. First, Jesus defines sex outside of marriage as sinful:

> For out of the heart come evil thoughts, murder, adultery, sexual immorality, theft, false witness, slander. These are what defile a person. (Matt. 15:19–20)

Jesus is saying that it is all too possible to be defiled, to be spiritually unacceptable to God. The Pharisees he is talking to generally believed that defilement was a bit like catching a cold: provided you avoided infected people and places, you could stay healthy. So they went to great lengths to wash themselves ceremonially and to stay away from people they thought were spiritually unclean. But Jesus shows them that defilement is not primarily something external to us but internal. It is not outside of us and to be avoided, but inside of us and to be acknowledged—it comes *out of the heart*. Various attitudes and types of behavior reflect this, and Jesus provides a sampling of them:

evil thoughts, murder, adultery, sexual immorality, theft, false witness, and slander.

This is not an exhaustive list but a representative one. And in the middle of it comes the phrase "sexual immorality." It is a translation of one Greek word, *porneia*, which is what Matthew originally wrote. If that word sounds a little familiar, it is because we get the word *pornography* from it. At the time of Jesus, *porneia* referred to any sexual behavior outside of marriage. It would have included premarital sex, prostitution, adultery (which Jesus also lists separately), and same-sex behavior. Such sexual activity, Jesus says, defiles us. It is not the only form of behavior that does (as the rest of his list indicates), but it is one of the things. Sex outside of marriage is a sin. In other words, what, I suspect, is the vast majority of sexual behavior in our culture today, Jesus regards as morally wrong. He's not so sexually tolerant, as it happens.

But Jesus's teaching is even more challenging than that. In his famous Sermon on the Mount, Jesus included these words:

> You have heard that it was said, "You shall not commit adultery." But I say to you that everyone who looks at a woman with lustful intent has already committed adultery with her in his heart. (Matt. 5:27–28)

In this section of the Sermon on the Mount, Jesus is contrasting the traditions of the religious teachers at that time with the heart attitude that God intends his laws to promote and his people to have. Evidently it was common to teach the law primarily in terms of externals, so Jesus shows that it was always meant to go much deeper. It is not enough, he shows us, merely to refrain from physically committing adultery. What God requires is honorable intentions and a godly attitude. It is not just about what we *do* (or manage not to do) but what and even how we *think*. Jesus doesn't take the Old Testament law and go easy on his hearers; he dials it up for them.

One more passage reflects this:

> And Pharisees came up to him and tested him by asking, "Is it lawful to divorce one's wife for any cause?" He answered, "Have you not read that he who created them from the beginning made them male and female, and said, 'Therefore a man shall leave his father and his mother and hold fast to his wife, and the two shall become one flesh'? So they are no longer two but one flesh. What therefore God has joined together, let not man separate." (Matt. 19:3–6)

Jesus is asked about divorce, but his answer doesn't cover divorce. Instead he talks about marriage. To do that Jesus goes back to Genesis 1 and 2. When he says, "He who created them from the beginning made them male and female," he is referencing Genesis 1:27. Then he directly quotes Genesis 2:24: "Therefore a man shall leave . . ." But Jesus makes clear that by referencing these early chapters of Scripture, he is not merely seeking wisdom from the ancients. Notice it is "he who created them" who says, "Therefore a man shall leave his father and his mother and hold fast to his wife." It is the Creator himself who provides these words of commentary on what marriage is. What we are seeing is, therefore, the Creator's blueprint for human sexuality. This is not the best of human wisdom; it is our Maker's design for us.

That design clearly shows us that God's template for marriage is one man and one woman for life. This, Jesus shows us, is the union that alone enables two people to become "one flesh." This is not something designed to be undone or reversed. And as Jesus continues to unpack this, and its implications for how we think about divorce, the disciples respond in a telling way:

> The disciples said to him, "If such is the case of a man with
> his wife, it is better not to marry." (Matt. 19:10)

This is telling for a very simple reason. I've read these words
countless times over the years but only really noticed just recently that when Jesus talks about what marriage is, he actually
puts people *off* getting married. The disciples realize how serious
marriage is. *Maybe best to give it a miss*, they think. It sounds a
little too much like commitment. Their reaction is understandable, but it got me thinking. One of the perks of being a pastor
is that I get to preach at weddings fairly often. But never has
someone come up to me after I've preached on what marriage
is and means and said, "Maybe it is better not to marry." This
makes me wonder if it was *Jesus's* view of marriage I was actually teaching. His is not an easy standard when it comes to sex
and marriage.

Jesus's response to the disciples seems to underline this:

> But he said to them, "Not everyone can receive this saying,
> but only those to whom it is given." (Matt. 19:11)

There is discussion among scholars about whether "this saying"
refers to all that Jesus had just been teaching or to what the
disciples have just said in response to his teaching. If it is to the
former, Jesus is underlining how the Christian standard for marriage will not be for all; hence what he says next about the life
of celibacy as the alternative. If Jesus is referring to the latter—
to the disciples' remark about it being better not to marry—he is
saying that not all will be able to follow the way of life they are
commending, although some do and hence the comments about
eunuchs. Concerning one way, it is the Christian view of marriage that will be hard to accept; concerning the other, it is the
Christian view of singleness that will be hard to accept.

In one sense, it doesn't make much difference. The fact is, marriage can be hard and so too can singleness. Each brings its own challenges. Neither option is the easier one, and the challenges of marriage are quite different from the challenges of singleness. But I suggest Jesus is referring to what he has just been teaching. It is a hard word for many to hear and receive.[2]

If the disciples had hoped the strength of their reaction might make Jesus equivocate in some way, his response would have felt like a slap in the face. Jesus doesn't soften his stance. He tacitly agrees with what they say about marriage.[3] It's difficult. So what's the answer? Interestingly, it's not cohabitation.

It's celibacy.

Jesus continues:

> For there are eunuchs who have been so from birth, and there are eunuchs who have been made eunuchs by men, and there are eunuchs who have made themselves eunuchs for the sake of the kingdom of heaven. (Matt. 19:12)

Eunuchs were celibate men in Jesus's day, particularly those who had been emasculated. Jesus goes on to show that some were eunuchs involuntarily: they were born that way or made that way by others. But alongside that, some were willing to forgo marriage by choice. Barry Danylak notes, "In using the term eunuch, Jesus meant more than someone simply not marrying but rather one's setting aside the right of marriage and procreation. . . . Jesus is suggesting that there are some who will willingly give up the blessings of both marriage and offspring for the sake of the kingdom of God."[4] We will think more about this in due course, but for now we can simply note this: when the disciples raise the possibility of not getting married, Jesus talks to them about being eunuchs. As far as he is concerned, that is the only godly alternative to marriage.

These are all challenging statements, but they are very clear. To summarize these three passages:

- Sex outside of marriage is sinful (Matt. 15:19).

- Sexual sin includes not just the physical act, but our thoughts and attitudes too (Matt. 5:28).

- Marriage is between a man and a woman, for life, and the godly alternative is to be celibate (Matt. 19:4–5, 10–12).

Jesus is therefore not as sexually tolerant as people today commonly imagine him to be. Far from relaxing the common Jewish traditions on sexual ethics derived from the Old Testament, he actually intensifies them. For those wanting to follow him, being unmarried very much involves singleness with sexual abstinence.

The Goodness of Singleness

That may clarify the terms of our discussion. But we still haven't answered our central concern: Is biblical singleness too hard? Look again at Jesus's exchange with his disciples following his teaching on marriage and divorce:

> The disciples said to him, "If such is the case of a man with his wife, it is better not to marry." But he said to them, "Not everyone can receive this saying, but only those to whom it is given. For there are eunuchs who have been so from birth, and there are eunuchs who have been made eunuchs by men, and there are eunuchs who have made themselves eunuchs for the sake of the kingdom of heaven." (Matt. 19:10–12)

Notice again the disciples' premise: marriage sounds too hard. Jesus doesn't contradict that. Marriage (as he presents it) is not easy. It *is* hard. It will not be the best path for everyone. That is why some choose to be like the eunuchs. Our starting point today is often the opposite. Celibacy sounds too hard, so we should make marriage more readily accessible, even redefining it so that more people can enter into it. But Jesus's thinking seems to go in the opposite direction. Marriage can be too hard for some, so he commends celibacy.

We also need to remember that Jesus made himself a eunuch for the sake of the kingdom. Jesus willingly became fully human for us. He willingly became a male. He was a sexual human being, as we all are. But he lived a celibate lifestyle. He never married. He never even entered a romantic relationship. He never had sex. Jesus was not calling others to a standard he was not willing to embrace himself. He wasn't calling singles to sexual abstinence while knowing nothing of it himself. He lived this very teaching.

But there's more than even that. Jesus is not just an example of a nonhypocritical teacher. He is the example of the perfect man. He is the humanity all of us are called to be but which none of us are. He is the most complete and fully human person who ever lived. So his not being married is not incidental. It shows us that none of these things—marriage, romantic fulfillment, sexual experience—is intrinsic to being a full human being. The moment we say otherwise, the moment we claim a life of celibacy to be dehumanizing, we are implying that Jesus himself is only subhuman.

The significance of this came home to me recently. I was speaking to a pastor who was expressing reservations about calling same-sex-attracted members of his church to the sexual ethic we have just been outlining. He summarized his concern with these words: "How can I expect them to live without romantic hope?" I was grateful for his concern for them. Many married pastors can be blasé about what they're asking of some of their unmarried church members. He, at least, was aware of the potential cost for them, and it mattered to him. But there was an assumption behind his concern that troubled me. The assumption was that we can't really live without romantic hope, that a life without any potential for romantic fulfillment is unfair to demand and unbearable to experience. It assumes romantic fulfillment is fundamental to a full and complete life.

Some time later I was preaching from 1 John and found myself teaching a passage that includes these words:

> By this you know the Spirit of God: every spirit that confesses that Jesus Christ has come in the flesh is from God, and every spirit that does not confess Jesus is not from God. This is the spirit of the antichrist, which you heard was coming and now is in the world already. (1 John 4:2–3)

There was an opportunity for questions from the congregation after the sermon, and someone asked whether there is, in fact, anyone today who denies that Christ has come in the flesh. Wasn't that just a first-century heresy that the early church was able to see off? I was thinking for a moment about how to respond when I suddenly remembered that conversation with the pastor. It dawned on me that the very kind of thinking that claims a life without sexual fulfillment is not really an authentic way to live is actually saying that Jesus did not fully come in the flesh, that his was not a full human life. To say that it is dehumanizing to be celibate is to dehumanize Christ, to deny that he came fully in the flesh and that his humanity was a "real" one.

A couple of times when I've spoken on this issue, people have questioned whether Jesus really was celibate. The Gospel accounts don't explicitly say that Jesus didn't have sex, so it's a bit much to forbid others to do so on that basis. I've even heard some senior church leaders in my own denomination say this.

It is a rather unusual approach to say that anything we're not told Jesus didn't do can be morally justified. There is no account in any of the Gospels of Jesus, say, punching a horse in the face. But the fact that the Gospels don't say he didn't do it doesn't make me think I can thereby justify doing it myself. If someone responds to this (admittedly daft) example, that such behavior doesn't fit with the Jesus we see in the Gospels, then I'd reply that this is precisely the point. It doesn't. It is absurd to think of Jesus behaving this way. And the same is true of the notion that he might have had sex. This, after all, is the man (as we've seen) who presented a much higher standard of sexual ethics to his contemporaries than was commonly taught. Are we to think that Jesus would have explicitly and repeatedly taught one thing while doing the opposite? Quite apart from this is the constant reminder throughout the New Testament (very much reflected in the Gospel accounts) that Jesus lived without sin.

So far, all we've really done is see how high is Jesus's standard for sexual ethics and how his teaching on marriage makes it much harder than we might typically think. Hardly encouraging stuff. But the message of the Bible about singleness is much more than this. Paul is able to express ways in which singleness can be a good thing. There are ways in which it can actually be easier than marriage. He puts it both ways around: there are certain hardships we are spared if we are single and certain ways in which we are more free because of it.

Let's deal with what we're spared. Writing to the Corinthians, Paul shows how Christians are both free to marry and free to remain single. Though he is single and wants to commend his singleness to them (1 Cor. 7:7), there is nothing wrong with single people who are able to marry getting married:

> But if you do marry, you have not sinned, and if a betrothed woman marries, she has not sinned. Yet those who marry will have worldly troubles, and I would spare you that. (1 Cor. 7:28)

Paul assumes that married life will include certain "worldly troubles." This is by no means a criticism of marriage. Elsewhere Paul writes in the loftiest of terms about how marriage reflects the church's spiritual marriage to Jesus (Eph. 5:31). It is not that Paul is down on marriage. It's just that he is realistic. The character of life in this world is that marriage will not be easy. There will be some heartache that comes with it.

It's important for us to know this. From the earliest of ages we have been presented with the idea that the period following marriage is best described as "happily ever after." While most of us know enough to realize life isn't as simple as that, the fact is, we are exposed to endless stories as adults where the wedding is the end and climax, the resolution of the tension. It is the goal and destination. Once the couple finally gets together, the story is over. While not *entirely* "happily ever after," it seems at least *mainly* "happily ever after."

I've been a pastor for about fifteen years, and a close friend to various married folks for a lot longer. I have seen a number of marriages at close hand and walked with married friends through some of the trials that have come with married life. It is good to have open and honest friendships in which both the ups *and* downs can be shared.

There are some "worldly troubles" caused by marriage itself.

One of the first couples at whose wedding I officiated has now divorced. I know of several marriages going through very serious problems. One friend was recently quite candid with me: he and his wife simply don't like each other anymore.

I know couples for whom married life turned out dramatically different from how they'd expected. One lady with a long-term incapacitated husband said to me one day, "This isn't what I signed up for!" (*Actually it is*, I thought, but didn't say.) I know another couple in which the husband has a condition that has dramatically weakened his arms. He is unable to button his own shirts, let alone lift his own children—a far cry from how he had imagined being a husband. I know of a Christian who married someone who wasn't, and though she thought it wouldn't matter, it has turned out to matter profoundly. I know another case in which a woman married someone who presented himself as a strong Christian but has shown himself to be far from it.

Other "worldly troubles" relate to children. I've seen friends devastated by the news that they will not be able to have children. Suddenly all the expectations they had about what family life might look like for them came crashing down. Though they have had the blessing of being able to adopt multiple times, and regard their children as full family members, they know that the grandparents will never be able to say of their children, "He definitely has your eyes!" or "She has the family nose!"

More than one couple I'm very close to has had children born with special needs and gone through the deep distress of not even knowing if these children were going to survive their first few days in the world. Other couples I know have experienced the searing pain of seeing a child stumble into serious sin or walk away from the faith entirely. One very dear family I know lost one daughter to cancer and another to suicide.

I could go on. The point of all this is that there are both ups *and* downs in married life and that these are all griefs that, as a single person, I will never directly experience. That is not to be taken lightly. I will experience a measure of these pains as I seek to walk closely with friends through such times, but that is not the same as having to directly face these difficulties myself.

None of this is to put us off marriage or to imply that it is simple a litany of woes. It is a gift from God and not to be despised. Paul describes those who forbid getting married as teaching the "teachings of demons" (1 Tim. 4:1–3). Marriage is intrinsically good. But like all good things in a fallen world, it is tarnished by sin and not without problems.

The fact is, both singleness and marriage have their own particular ups and downs. The temptation for many who are single is to compare the downs of singleness with the ups of marriage. And the temptation for some married people is to compare the downs of marriage with the ups of singleness, which is equally dangerous. The grass will often seem greener on the other side. Whichever gift we have—marriage or singleness—the other can easily seem far more attractive. Paul's point is to show singles that there are some downs unique to marriage—some "worldly troubles"—that we are spared by virtue of our singleness. Our common assumption—marriage is better or easier—is simply not true. Seeing what I have seen in the last decade or so, I have to say I would choose the lows of singleness over the lows of marriage any day of the week. I think being unhappily married must be so much harder than being unhappily single.

But as well as the absence of some problems, Paul also talks about the presence of certain opportunities. Singleness is not just about what we're spared but about what we're given.

> I want you to be free from anxieties. The unmarried man is anxious about the things of the Lord, how to please the Lord. But the married man is anxious about worldly things, how to please his wife, and his interests are divided. And the unmarried or betrothed woman is anxious about the things of the Lord, how to be holy in body and spirit. But the married woman is anxious about worldly things, how to please her husband. I say this for your own benefit, not to lay any restraint upon you, but to promote good order and to secure your undivided devotion to the Lord. (1 Cor. 7:32–35)

If we are not careful, it is easy to misunderstand this passage. Paul is not saying that singleness is spiritual and marriage unspiritual. Nor is he saying that singleness is easy but marriage is hard. No, the contrast is between complexity and simplicity. Married life is more complicated; singleness is more straightforward.

Paul reminds us of something of the character of marriage: both the husband and the wife are "anxious about worldly things." Paul does not mean that in a pejorative sense. He is not saying that their focus is on ungodly things. He is saying that for the husband or wife, much of their attention is on the things of this world. This is at it should be. The husband and wife have a duty to each other and to any children. They are to think about how they can love and encourage each other. They are to be mindful of each other's spiritual, emotional, and physical needs as well as those of any children they may have. The concerns of the married man or woman are split because of this. Life can easily feel like a swirl of immediate, pressing, and competing needs. Married people by necessity are engrossed in the things of this world. To live and act otherwise would be a dereliction of their responsibilities.

For the single person, there is greater freedom. Our focus is less divided. Life is less complicated. We are able to give of ourselves in a way that married people are not. Paul is no doubt thinking of some of the ways he has seen this freedom in his own life and ministry. He has been able to travel widely, to spend extended periods of time in particular places, even risking his life for the cause of the gospel. None of this would have been the case if he was married.

Paul is not saying that married people have concerns and single people do not, but that those concerns are necessarily different. The single life is not meant to be free of all responsibilities. We still have friendships and family that we need to honor. But as Vaughan Roberts writes, "we are pulled in fewer directions than those who are married and are therefore free to give more time to 'the Lord's affairs.'"[5] Our lives as single people are generally less complicated than those of our married friends.

I was talking to a married friend about some travel I had coming up. There was going to be a lot of long-haul flying. He immediately winced at the thought of it. I looked puzzled.

"Don't you just *hate* flying?" he asked.

"No, I love it. I get so much work done. All those hours uninterrupted. I do some of my best studying and thinking on planes."

"Yes, I keep forgetting: you don't have children with you when you fly."

Although this is a fairly trivial example, it made me realize that even in some of the mundane details of life, he and I see things from very different perspectives. Travel for me (especially on long flights) represents an opportunity to get lots of things done. For him, it represents finding ways to keep some small energetic people occupied for hours at a time. Apply that to many parts of life, and it becomes clear that life for me is much less complicated.

There are dangers that come with this, of course. Paul is assuming we singles will be "anxious about the things of the Lord." This is a battle for many of us. It is easy to channel our flexibility and energies into merely pleasing ourselves rather than God. A significant temptation for many singles, especially if we live on our own, is to become self-centered. I can easily become anxious about "the things of me." It is easy to do what I want, how I want, when I want. I don't have a "significant other" to have to flex around. If I want to go out, I can. If I want to have some space for myself, I can. For us singles it is much easier to eat when we want and sleep when we want. We need to remind ourselves, daily, that our singleness is not for us but for the Lord. It's not for our concerns, but for his.

I'm reminded of this when I stay with others. As I mentioned, I tend to travel a lot these days, and where I can, I try to stay in friends' homes rather than in hotels. I prefer this not only for the company but because it gives me a set of people to whom I have to adjust. I might need to be home by a given time to fit in with family mealtimes. There might be chores to help with. I can't simply take over the living room and binge-watch TV if I'm feeling tired and antisocial. Even if it is just for a few days, living with others is—in all the right ways—inconvenient.

None of this is to say that singleness is easy or that it is necessarily easier than marriage. It is simply to say that we are wrong to assume singleness is too hard. To do so easily overlooks the many ways in which marriage can be very difficult. It is not for nothing that the disciples said, "It is better not to marry." There are some specific "worldly troubles" that come with married life. We must not overlook the ways in which singleness frees us up for undivided devotion to Jesus. It is easy to think of singleness as a burden, a constraint, restricting us from real life. Paul says the opposite:

> I say this for your own benefit, not to lay any restraint upon you, but to promote good order and to secure your undivided devotion to the Lord. (1 Cor. 7:35)

Paul does not want to restrain us—literally, "to throw a noose around you." We all too readily assume that is precisely what he *is* doing. Singleness, for him, is not primarily about what we do without (except for the "worldly troubles" that come with married life) but rather what we are free to do. He is commending singleness because he wants "good order," the advantage of a more orderly, less complex way of living, which itself enables us to wholeheartedly serve the Lord.

2

Singleness Requires a Special Calling

It is July, which in movie terms means we're well into superhero season. Everywhere you look, there is the usual circus of sequels, reboots, sequels of reboots, and crossover movies bringing together characters from all the above, and then sequels of the crossover movies, which will then at some point presumably be rebooted. I just saw the latest version of *Spider-man*, someone who recently seems to have gone through more incarnations than the Buddha. It's hard to avoid the impression that reboots are basically a studio admitting that even after several $100-million-plus attempts, they still don't quite know how to turn some drawings into a movie. Yet we evidently keep lapping it up. Virtually all this summer's biggest hits have been superhero movies.

It is easy to see the appeal. We've always been drawn to superheroes. I suspect the Old Testament book Judges has something to do with it. As a recent book reminds us, our popular-cultural narratives both "long for and echo the truth" God has given us.[1]

In Judges we see that part of the template God has given us of salvation involves the raising up of specially endowed individuals to come in and save the day. And, just like our modern-day superheroes, none of these figures alone seems able to cut it. Each has his own limitations and flaws, so more are successively introduced to pick up where the previous one left off, without ever giving the people what they ultimately need. This process in Judges shows us that we really need someone to come who (1) is not deeply flawed, and (2) death will not take from us. And it shows us why we seem wired to want superheroes.

Just as the concept of a superhero dominates the summer box office, it can easily dominate the way we think about the biblical idea of singleness. Again, many of our default settings see singleness in terms of deficiency. It is the absence of a good thing—marriage, and the romantic and sexual fulfillment marriage seems to represent. Single people are *unmarried*, while we would never think of married people as *unsingle*. It is singleness that seems to be wanting and deficient. The only way to cope with it is if God gives you some special superpower.

All of this means we can find ourselves quite out of sync with how Paul describes singleness in the New Testament. He speaks of singleness not just as being bearable but as being a *gift* from God:

> I wish that all were as I myself am. But each has his own gift from God, one of one kind and one of another. (1 Cor. 7:7)

Paul has just been talking about marriage, specifically the obligation married people have to serve one another sexually (1 Cor. 7:3–5). So when he says, "I wish that all were as I myself am," it is very clear what he is talking about. He is not saying he wishes all people were male or from Tarsus or called "Paul"; he's saying there's a sense in which he wishes all people were like him in his singleness. There are certain benefits and even advantages to it (which he'll get to later in this passage). In one sense it'd be great if all believers were single. But that's not how God has ordered and arranged things: "Each has his own gift from God, one of one kind and one of another." While singleness is good, it is not God's purpose for everyone to remain single. Each has his or her own gift, meaning that each is either single (like Paul) or else married. His point is that both marriage and singleness are gifts, as far as Paul's concerned. Marriage is a gift, and so too is singleness.

Most of us know someone who fails spectacularly to understand what we actually enjoy. (I once received a gift from a local friend so bad that it meant having to leave it at a thrift shop in another town to avoid the risk of the giver coming across it and realizing what I'd done.)

But while single people may chuckle at the idea of God giving such a potentially unwanted gift, we need to be careful and recognize what and who it is we're laughing at. God is no fool. He is not the uncle who still thinks you're twelve when you're well into your thirties and sends you childish gifts. He is the Creator who made you and knows you. He is the One who orders all things and does so for your good. To roll our eyes at what a well-meaning but mistaken relative gives us is one thing; to roll our eyes at omniscience is another. If we balk at the idea of singleness being a gift, it is not because God has not understood us but because we have not understood him.

So what does this mean? What is the *gift* of singleness?

The Nature of the Gift

Given what we've already seen about the negative ways in which singleness has been viewed, many Christians have taken "the gift of singleness" to mean some special capacity to cope with it. It's an unusual endowment that enables certain chosen people to survive as single. It's like a superpower.

And, like a superpower, we presume it must be rare and unusual. The whole point of superheroes is that their powers are abnormal. That's part of the appeal. They are set apart from the rest of us. And so those with the gift of singleness must be a select group who can cope with singleness in a way the rest of us cannot. It seems to fit what Paul is saying and to fit our experience of what singleness is like. But there are a number of problems with this way of thinking.

1. It is ultimately another way of denying the intrinsic goodness of singleness. Think about it: if singleness requires a special spiritual superpower just to survive it, it must be really terrible. Al Hsu compares the gift of singleness to anesthesia during surgery: "Between the lines is the idea that nobody would ever make a conscious choice to stay single if he or she had the opportunity to marry."[2] This reinforces a number of common and faulty ways of thinking, that a life without marriage is not really life to the full, and therefore that people desirous of such a life, even if for the sake of the kingdom, are ultimately choosing something quite unhealthy. Singleness, in and of itself, has nothing good going for it and so requires a special "gift" to make it bearable.

2. It can encourage bitterness rather than the pursuit of godly contentment. For those who are single and unhappily so, this thinking can be a way of writing off the contentment others may have in being single—"they obviously have the gift of singleness, whereas I don't."

3. It unwittingly permits disobedience. What if certain singles are convinced they don't have the gift of singleness yet find

themselves in a situation where the only opportunities for a romantic relationship involve sin? Imagine they have always been exclusively same-sex attracted, or that they are in a context where there are simply no eligible Christians of the opposite sex to marry. What is the answer? Either way, God seems to have gotten something wrong. And if the choice is rejecting the idea that they don't have the gift of singleness after all, or rejecting the idea that same-sex or spiritually mixed partnerships are wrong, I know which they will most likely choose. I've seen it time and again. I think of a woman who married a non-Christian, justifying it, because "I know God doesn't want me to be unmarried." I think of another individual whose rationale for getting involved in a same-sex partnership was, "I'm not called to celibacy," and so effectively had no other choice. Notice in both cases it is ultimately God's fault. He puts us in a situation where we have no capacity to obey him.

But we know this is not how our loving heavenly Father works. He is one. He is perfectly integrated in all he is and says and does. His Word is never contradictory. Acceptance of one part of it never, ever involves denying another part of it. Obeying one word never involves disobeying another. To think any situation necessitates sin denies the perfect unity and integrity of God. It makes him like us, inconsistent and contradictory. It also denies his goodness, suggesting he is in the habit of stitching us up: calling us to do something and then withholding all ability to do it.

4. It is hard to see why someone should not apply the same logic to marriage. I know one or two people right now who are really unhappily married. One, Steve (not his real name), and his wife exist together solely as coparents of their children. They don't have a friendship of their own anymore. They don't even

like each other. It is easy for him to spend as much time away from home as he can. He is in Christian ministry and can therefore fill up his evenings and weekends with work to avoid what is a horrible situation at home. I know he looks on my singleness with enormous envy. What is to stop him from concluding, "I'm married, but I clearly don't have the *gift* of marriage and therefore I need to leave my family"? This would be "tantamount to calling God the cause of divorce."[3] If there is a "gift of singleness" that enables only some to thrive as single people, there is no reason to say there is no corresponding "gift of marriage" that enables only some married people to thrive in their marriages.

The fact is, marriage is not easy. Thinking that singleness uniquely requires a special gift masks the extent to which marriage is also very challenging to sinners like us. It is not for nothing that the Book of Common Prayer warns that marriage is "not by any to be enterprised, nor taken in hand, unadvisedly, lightly, or wantonly; but reverently, discreetly, advisedly, soberly, and in the fear of God."

5. Tim Keller also points out that this way of thinking about gifts does not fit with Paul's teaching more generally:

> In his writings, Paul always uses the word "gift" to mean an ability God gives to build others up. Paul is not speaking . . . of some kind of elusive, stress-free state.[4]

Gifts (as Paul will go on to explain later in his letter to the Corinthians) are about building up the church rather than feeling a sense of individual, personal fulfillment. It is about serving others and not about feeling a special sense of peace. Keller continues:

> The "gift-ness" of being single for Paul lay in the freedom it gave him to concentrate on ministry in ways that a married

man could not. Paul may very well, then, have experienced what we today would call an "emotional struggle" with singleness. He might have wanted to be married. He not only found an ability to live a life of service to God and others in that situation, he discovered (and capitalized on) the unique features of the single life (such as time flexibility) to minister with very great effectiveness.[5]

The Goodness of the Gift

This is good news. As Vaughan Roberts says, it means that "none of us is missing out."[6] All of us get something of the goodness of God. It doesn't deny that there are challenges with both marriage and singleness. But it serves to remind us that, even in the midst of those challenges, we can taste something of the goodness of God. It protects us from the kind of despair that comes from thinking we've been locked into something that is utterly unbearable, or that God has made a huge mistake.

What Paul says next in 1 Corinthians 7 also seems, at first glance, to reinforce the idea that singleness requires a special calling or gifting:

> To the unmarried and the widows I say that it is good for them to remain single, as I am. But if they cannot exercise self-control, they should marry. For it is better to marry than to burn with passion. (vv. 8–9)

This hardly sounds romantic. Paul seems to be saying that if you struggle to control your sexual or romantic yearnings, then you should marry. It is hard to imagine a guy saying this on bended knee while proffering a ring to his girlfriend: "I've been struggling to exercise self-control as a single person, so I think I should marry rather than be aflame with passion." It sounds as though Paul just sees marriage as a kind of release for uncontrollable sexual passion. It makes me think of those ramps they have on steeply descending roads for runaway trucks. If your sexual feelings are barreling out of control, then just swerve off into marriage and that'll take care of it. It is all a far cry from the Paul who wrote the timeless paean to love in 1 Corinthians 13, which has become one of the most celebrated parts of Scripture; or from the Paul who could speak with such breathtaking grandeur about marriage being a picture of the relationship between Christ and the church.

And yet this is surely part of the point. What Paul says here is not the only thing he has to say about marriage. He's not pretending to provide here an exhaustive list of all that needs to be considered when choosing whether or whom to marry. His point is much more specific: if all other things are equal, then an overwhelming desire for sexual intimacy may be a reason to think about choosing to marry.

And this needs to be considered alongside the other things Scripture says about how we go about finding an appropriate marriage partner. Not everyone struggling to exercise self-control in this area will necessarily be able to find someone appropriate to marry. The presence of significant sexual desires does not justify disobeying other biblical commands about, say, not marrying someone of the same sex or someone who does not share our faith in Christ. We can't just take 1 Corinthians 7:9 on its own and deduce from it that God now somehow owes us some form of sexual intimacy. Paul's point is that those who can marry appropriately are free to and, if their sexual desires risk distracting them from a wholehearted focus on the Lord, are encouraged to.

It helps to bear in mind how many people in Paul's time thought about these things. The ancient world tended to separate marriage from romantic or sexual fulfillment. Marriage was about matching up with someone of appropriate economic and social status and securing heirs. It was about business and posterity. For sexual or romantic fulfillment you turned not to your wife but to a concubine or a lover (and often to both). Paul's point is that you should turn to marriage to fulfill your passions not because he thinks that's all marriage is good for, but because marriage is the only godly place for such passions to be fulfilled.

The alternative to all this, according to Paul, is to "burn." Needless to say, lots of trees have been felled in discussions about what exactly this means, but New Testament theologian and historian Paul Barnett seems to have the best analysis:

> In mind here is the "heat" of sexual passion which is absorbed, softened and cooled within the intimacy of the marriage commitment. Otherwise it would "burn" out of control, bringing destruction to all parties. But there may be at the same time a deeper meaning. Paul is thinking of "burning" as an image for hell fire. . . . It is easy to mock medieval images of hell. Yet the reality of eternal separation from God, which the image of fire portrays, is truly awesome.[7]

This certainly fits the wider context of this passage. Just two chapters earlier Paul has reminded us of the seriousness of sexual sin:

> It is actually reported that there is sexual immorality among you, and of a kind that is not tolerated even among pagans, for a man has his father's wife. And you are arrogant! Ought you not rather to mourn? Let him who has done this be removed from among you. (1 Cor. 5:1–2)

Sin matters. And that means sexual sin matters. It calls for mourning, and even (in some cases) severe church discipline.

So it is not as simple as to say that anyone experiencing ongoing sexual tension must get married. Otherwise, as Vaughan Roberts says, "many would need to get married at puberty."[8]

Two problems arise if we continue to think about singleness as being a special kind of calling. First, it will make large numbers of single people feel as though life hasn't started yet. They're single but don't perceive themselves as having "the gift" of singleness. They're in a situation they're not designed for or called to. Life feels as though it is in limbo until God notices he's accidentally "misfiled" us as being single and fixes things. *That's* when things will feel like they've finally got going, but until then we're just kicking about.

Second, it can lead to undue pressure to get married, especially for those single people not perceived to have that gift. If you're single and don't have the "gift of singleness," then you're not pulling your weight. You should be married by now.

One prominent Christian leader recently made the following remarks about singleness:

> Let me tell you the most devastating attack on marriage today is coming from singleness. Singleness is an assault on marriage. Marriage is the grace of life. As a pastor, I tell my people, "Look, if it keeps going this way, I'm gonna line all the girls on one side, all the guys on the other, we're gonna just match you up and have a huge wedding." This escalating self-preoccupation, personal ambition, personal development . . . that creates a kind of terminal singleness is devastating on obviously the family. . . . I just see singleness as a disaster.[9]

The speaker is expressing a godly concern, albeit in very poorly chosen language. Many people today are delaying marriage for entirely selfish reasons. Tim Keller identifies something of the same problem:

> Adults in Western society are deeply shaped by individualism, a fear and even hatred of limiting options for the sake of others. Many people are living single lives today not in the conscious lonely misery of wanting marriage too much but rather in the largely unconscious, lonely misery of wanting marriage too little, out of fear of it.[10]

That this is happening is incontrovertible. United States Senator Ben Sasse has recently described it as part of a wider trend for extending the lifestyle of adolescence well into adulthood.[11]

Yet the underlying problem is not with singleness, but with selfishness. That Christian speaker was wrong to suggest that singleness is a disaster. The issue is what singleness is being used for. To call singleness itself a "threat to marriage" is to speak about it in a profoundly unbiblical way that I am sure would astonish Paul. It is also possible to marry for lazy and selfish reasons rather than for godly ones, yet I doubt anyone would think to say that marriage itself is a "disaster." The issue is not the state of marriage or the state of singleness. Both are gifts. The issue is our heart and what is motivating us. We mustn't blame selfishly deferring marriage on singleness any more than we should blame selfishness in marriage on marriage itself.

This presents many pastors with a challenge, especially if they minister in contexts where there are large numbers of single people. There is a need to challenge those who defer marriage for ungodly reasons without demeaning those whose singleness is either not their choice or has in fact been chosen for the sake of the kingdom. There is also a need to affirm the goodness and advantages of singleness without unwittingly playing into selfish motivations of those for whom singleness seems easier.

Singleness, like marriage, is a good thing. It needs to be received appropriately and held in a biblical perspective, as does marriage. When we honor it, as God intends us to, as a good gift, then we won't presume it needs some spiritual superpower to make it bearable.

3

Singleness Means No Intimacy

It was the kind of email that breaks your heart.

A friend of mine, who lives too far away, contacted me to say he was struggling to understand how the cost of singleness as a Christian could possibly be worth it. As far as he could see, an illicit relationship would be "the only possible way for me to enjoy the relational intimacy I've dreamt of my entire life." He concluded, "I cannot imagine the shell of a life I would live without somebody standing by my side." In the light of this deficit of intimacy, could singleness ever be worth it?

My friend isn't alone. In my own church family, one of the biggest causes of people drifting away from Christ has been entering into illicit relationships. For many of them, the assumption was that life as a single just isn't viable. They needed intimacy.

It has become an unquestioned assumption today: singleness (biblically conceived) and intimacy are alternatives. A choice to be celibate is a choice to be alone. No wonder for so many this seems too much to bear. Can we really expect someone to live without romantic hope? It sounds so unfair.

As we have seen, the Bible is clear that the alternative to marriage is celibacy. When his disciples started to get cold feet about marriage, Jesus made clear to them that the only godly alternative was to be like the eunuchs, to be sexually abstinent (Matt. 19:10–12).

But the choice between marriage and celibacy is not the choice between intimacy and loneliness, or at least it shouldn't be. We can manage without sex. We know this—Jesus himself lived as a celibate man. So did Paul. Many others have done so as well. But we are not designed to live without intimacy. Marriage is not the sole answer to the observation, "It is not good that the man should be alone" (Gen. 2:18).

Rethinking Intimacy

So why doesn't this seem to be the case? A significant part of this has to do with how we tend to think about intimacy today. In the West, we have virtually collapsed sex and intimacy into each other. Where you have one, you are assumed to have the other. We can't really conceive of genuine intimacy without its being ultimately sexual.

We do not need to look far to see evidence of this. A couple of years ago in the United Kingdom, we commemorated the centenary of the outbreak of the First World War. As part of the commemorations there was a radio series featuring extracts from the diaries and letters of some of the soldiers. One of the aspects that came through was the depth of friendship that developed between many of them, forged and strengthened no doubt by the horrors they experienced together. This in itself was fascinating. But what stood out to me was the reaction of some of the people commenting on these extracts: "Well, they were obviously *gay*." Obviously, because they had deep affection, and deep affection must at root be sexual.

C. S. Lewis as ever hits the nail on the head: "Those who cannot conceive Friendship as substantive love but only as a disguise or elaboration of Eros betray the fact that they have never had a friend."[1] That our culture imagines that intimacy occurs only in the context of sexual attraction goes to show how little our culture actually understands and really experiences true friendship.

The Bible gives us a very different perspective. Intimacy and sex, while often overlapping, are not identical, nor are they always concurrent. It is possible to have a lot of sex and no intimacy. King David may well be an example of that. Consider these words of grief expressed by David after the death of his close friend Jonathan:

> I am distressed for you, my brother Jonathan;
>> very pleasant have you been to me;
> your love to me was extraordinary,
>> surpassing the love of women. (2 Sam. 1:26)

Hearing those words today, many people roll their eyes. Ed Shaw comments, "Today it seems impossible for anyone to read this song without thinking that David and Jonathan must have enjoyed a sexual relationship. Didn't you find yourself quickly sniffing out something homoerotic about them?"[2] But this is neither necessary nor even likely.

What we know of David's life and exploits sheds light on this. At the time he lamented the loss of his friend Jonathan, David had three wives (see 1 Sam. 25:42–44). His relationships with women were deeply complicated. The love of a woman, in David's experience, was far from straightforward. And so his delight in the closeness of Jonathan's friendship is easy to imagine. Ed Shaw asks, "Why is it not possible that he enjoyed the non-sexual intimacy of his friendship with Jonathan (also a married man) more than the sexual intimacy of his relationships with Abigail, Ahinoam and Michal?"[3]

David's words about the deep intimacy he enjoyed with Jonathan indicate not that it must have been sexual, but that the sexual relationships he had with the women in his life might have lacked real intimacy.

We see the same dynamic today. Hookup culture means that it can be very easy to have sex with someone you've only just met and barely know. It is a huge error to mistake this for true intimacy. Sexual union is designed to express and deepen intimacy within marriage. It cannot, in and of itself, create it from scratch. Yet we often sense that it is meant to, and can easily feel that pursuing sexual closeness will provide the deeper intimacy we are looking for. I've seen this a number of times in pastoral ministry. Within all of us is a deep yearning to know and be known. It can sometimes feel as though sex will deliver this. It seems to be a means of exposing who we are to someone else. After all, older generations used to use the language of "knowing" as a way to speak of having sex. But divorced from real relationship, sex may be a form of physical intimacy, but only that. It will not provide the deeper intimacy we need in life. It is possible to have lots of sex and no real intimacy.

But the reverse is also true. It is possible to have a lot of intimacy in life and for none of it to be sexual. Sexual and romantic relationships are not the only ones of genuine, life-giving closeness. We need to rediscover a biblical category of intimacy that has been neglected in our cultural context and sadly even in many of our churches—friendship.

Experiencing Intimacy in Friendship

The news has recently been preoccupied with speculation about the reasons for the breakup of a celebrity couple. The split was announced some time ago, but fresh allegations are emerging of infidelity, possibly by both of them. So the gossip mills are at full tilt wondering who some of the third parties might be.

We're fascinated with which celebrities might be sleeping together. We're not interested at all in which celebrities might be friends with one another. The former is newsworthy precisely because it is seen as having a higher order of significance. Sex is where real life happens. Friendship, on the other hand, has been hugely downgraded.

Think about it. In recent years "friend" has gone from being a noun to a verb, and a verb that describes something pretty mundane. We friend someone when we add them to our list of contacts on social media. To give someone access to our profile page is to make them a friend. Hardly surprising that for many of us today, a friend is little more than an acquaintance, someone we nominally stay in touch with and might meet up with from time to time.

But this is a massive downgrading of what friendship has meant to earlier generations, and what it continues to mean in many non-Western cultures today. There are a number of reasons for this downgrading, but not the least is that romantic and sexual relationships are now the primary place we look for any kind of intimacy, and all other forms of contact are relegated to a much lower place in our thinking.

Even sixty years ago, C. S. Lewis could see that friendship had become "something quite marginal; not a main course in life's banquet; a diversion; something that fills up the chink of one's time." He concluded, "Few value it because few experience it."[4] It is a trend that has continued right up to our own day. Christian theologian and writer Wesley Hill notes how the glut of recent "bromance" movies illustrates a deepening awkwardness many men in particular now feel about friendship:

> Films like *Superbad* and *I Love You, Man*, to choose only two of the recent array, show us the awkwardness of two men trying to achieve some kind of emotional closeness—to love each other, without saying the word—and at the same time avoid getting labeled as a couple. A tough gig, apparently.[5]

The sad reality is that there is now an appalling paucity of friendship in many of our churches. For our Western culture, and, sadly, for much of our church culture as well, friendship is largely dispensable. When it comes to intimacy, our focus is on the romantic and the marital. But this is all a far cry from what the Bible has in mind when it talks about friendship.

Take the book of Proverbs, for example. Here we find a high view of friendship. Consider this:

> A man of many companions may come to ruin,
>   but there is a friend who sticks closer than a brother.
>   (Prov. 18:24)

This seems diametrically opposed to the sort of way we typically think about friendship today. For many of us, friendship is kind of disposable. Friends are the people we hang around with for the season of life when we and they happen to be together. Proverbs is talking about something much more vital. The writer contrasts real friendship with two other kinds of relationship.

First, the friend is differentiated from what the proverb calls a "companion." The proverb assumes there are plenty of these around, and it seems to mean those who are more like familiar acquaintances rather than true friends. In other words, in life there are generally a good number of folk around who know us and are familiar with us, but who might not prove to be the people to count on when the chips are down. Actually, this is the exact category of people we tend to mean when we talk about friendship today—people we hang around with a fair bit but are not necessarily people we would open the deep things of our heart to. These are people who tend to come and go.

I think of old schoolmates, guys I spent a huge amount of time with. On one level we all knew each other quite well. I could tell you who they'd dated, or some of the legendarily stupid things they had said or done, or what they liked, or what they were and weren't good at. We had endless stories to tell about one another. But it was all rather trivial. I could tell you all those things about them, but I couldn't necessarily tell you what their great hopes and dreams were, or what they most feared in life. Maybe in one or two cases, but certainly not for many. They were companions of a sort—people who are around for company, people to do stuff with—but they're not what Proverbs is talking about.

Little wonder as we all moved on and moved away that we didn't really keep in touch. One or two I hear from. Occasionally someone resurfaces nearby, and we hang out a bit again. But by and large such people come and go as life moves on. We change jobs and acquire a new set of workmates. We move to a new area and find new neighbors. It's not realistic to keep up with all the old ones on top of getting to know new ones, so there's a sense of inevitability that as we move through different life stages and from one place to another, we tend to cycle through such relationships.

The writer of the proverb seems to assume we can have "many" such folk around. That is certainly more true today than it's ever been. Technology has made it easier than ever to have an abundance of companions. Social media keeps us in touch with dramatically more people than we could otherwise keep up with— all of those school friends and old work colleagues, the former neighbors, even people we've dated. Now we're still nominally in touch and kind of in the loop with *all* of them. I don't feel like I've lost touch when it takes all of three seconds to beam up their homepage and pretty much know exactly what they're up to.

But the danger is that this creates the illusion of true friendship without the actual reality of it. The average person has 237 Facebook friends, but what we have 237 of is far from what Proverbs would describe as "friends." You may have lots of people around who sort of know what you're up to, but that is a far cry from the soul-to-soul, spill-the-beans kind of friend that Proverbs is going to talk about. Having mates we can share time and have a laugh with is no bad thing, but in and of itself is not what Proverbs says we need in order to live well.

The other relationship contrasted to friendship is that of close family. The proverb makes a distinction between a friend and a brother. The two are not incompatible, of course. But in the ancient world family was hugely significant. It was very much the primary social unit you existed in, expressed loyalty to, and depended upon. And, of course, families are very often the ones who are there for us when the chips are down. But the proverb is highlighting a key distinction. One of the peculiar glories of friendship is its entirely voluntary nature. There is a sense in which families are obligated to one another by virtue of their common blood. Friends opt in to one another freely. A friend is someone who has *chosen* you. The obligation is entirely self-imposed, which can make it all the sweeter. As C. S. Lewis once put it, friendship is "the least *natural* of loves; the least instinctive, organic, biological, gregarious and necessary. . . . The species, biologically considered, has no need of it."[6] My friend Ray Ortlund makes the distinction in this way:

> A brother is stuck with you. A brother is obligated to be some kind of safety net. That is what family is for. But a friend chooses you. When someone loves you at all times, good and bad, and they don't have to but they choose to— that person is a friend.[7]

In our own day it might also help us to distinguish friendship from a third category of relationship—marriage. In some of the debates among Christians about same-sex relationships and the church, I've heard a number of people propose having some sort of "sexless marriage" for those who want to uphold the Christian sexual ethic while still having some sort of romantic partnership with another person of the same sex. This, they say, avoids the supposed loneliness of singleness while upholding biblical standards for sexual behavior.

The trouble with this kind of suggestion is that it implicitly assumes sex is the only main thing that separates marriage from other kinds of close friendship. This further underlines how we have misunderstood friendship and assumed "real" intimacy is in a sexual partnership.

Marriage is not just a close friendship with sex added. Nor is close friendship marriage without sex. Marriage, by definition and necessity, must be exclusive. It is covenantal. Friendship is not. My friendship with even a closest friend is not threatened by the growth of a similar friendship with someone else. It is not a zero-sum game. In fact, the opposite is often the case. A couple of years ago a close friend and I were planning a hiking trip to Scotland. I was really looking forward to it: one of my favorite people in one of my favorite places, doing one of my favorite activities. As the trip approached he suggested another friend of his come and join us. I was initially disappointed, having been looking forward to some time with just my friend and me. But having his other friend with us added so much. They'd been college roommates together, and this friend knew a whole side to my friend that I did not and brought out a whole side of him I hadn't seen before. It was better than it would have been had it been just the two of us. C. S. Lewis would not have been surprised:

> In each of my friends there is something that only some other friend can fully bring out. By myself I am not large enough to call the whole man into activity; I want other lights than my own to show all his facets. . . . Hence true friendship is the least jealous of loves.[8]

So Proverbs introduces us to a category of close relationship that is neither mere company nor kin. As we see what this friendship looks like, we realize it is dramatically different from what we tend to think of as friendship today. According to Proverbs, two particular features of real friendship stand out: it is not fleeting or superficial.

The Marks of Real Friendship

Real, true friendship is not fleeting:

A friend loves at all times,
    and a brother is born for adversity. (Prov. 17:17)

The sort of friendship we need in life has a constancy to it. Again, the contrast here is with the brother: a brother is born for adversity. That's when family really kicks in. We don't even need to think about it. When kin is in trouble, you show up.

Friendship is different. We mustn't misunderstand the contrast. It's not saying brothers are there for you in adversity in a way that friends aren't. It's saying friends are there for you *at all times* in a way that isn't necessarily the case with a biological brother. Brothers don't need to be especially close to be available in hard times. The relationship is not dependent on whether you have lots or little in common or how often you see each other. You're there when there's an emergency. But a friend is there always. There's constancy to friendship. Friends are there at all times, through thick and thin, rain and shine. No matter what. The sign of a real friend is that they're there for you in all seasons. That means they're there for you when you're at rock bottom:

> Wealth brings many new friends,
> but a poor man is deserted by his friend. (Prov. 19:4)

When we find good fortune, we're quickly surrounded by people who claim to be our friends. Lottery winners find they don't need to be the ones making the effort to keep in touch with people; everyone is in touch with them. Everyone comes out of the woodwork and reappears in life. But when there is a reversal of fortune, these "friends" go as quickly as they came.

We see this in Jesus's famous parable of the prodigal son. The son in the story demands his share of the inheritance from his father and moves far away to indulge himself. Newly wealthy and up for a good time, there was no short supply of company for him. But when the money was all gone and he was destitute, he had to resort to scavenging food from a pigsty because "no one gave him anything" (Luke 15:16). Everyone vanished when the wealth had gone. Lots of people are friendly when they think you're useful to them. They need you for something. The real friend doesn't see you as a means to an end, so they stick around. They don't just celebrate with you in your successes; they're there for you in your failures. Real friendship isn't fickle.

Real friendship also isn't superficial. A friend is not merely someone who knows your Facebook page. A friend is someone who knows your soul:

Oil and perfume make the heart glad,
and the sweetness of a friend comes from his earnest
counsel. (Prov. 27:9)

"His earnest counsel" literally translates as "the counsel of soul."[9] This counsel is not superficial advice but is deep and heartfelt. This is friendship operating at a soul-to-soul level, and there's nothing quite like it. A nice fragrance may do something to lift the spirits, but there is a particular sweetness to having an intimate friend give careful guidance to us. This is the case whether the counsel is positive or negative, easy to hear or deeply challenging. There is nothing like having a close friend, one of the people on earth who most knows and loves you, give you earnest direction in life.

Nearly twenty years ago I started dating a girl from our church. Everyone liked her, and then everyone seemed to like me just on account of the fact that I was dating her. Well, not quite everyone.

I was on a trip to southeast Asia with a team that included one of my best friends. We were sharing a room, and I vividly remember us both lying on our beds one night, staring up at the ceiling fan, while he gently but firmly told me why he wasn't impressed with my new relationship. It wasn't what I wanted to hear, but it was definitely what I needed to hear. It was a kind rebuke, a corrective to an attitude I shouldn't have been having. He gave me counsel from his soul, and I've remembered it ever since, precisely because it was an expression of the depth of our friendship and his concern for me. It had a sweetness to it. We've talked about it many times since. I think of it as one of the enduring highlights of our friendship, because it is a gift to have someone who knows your soul, knows the best and worst about you, yet through it all is deeply committed to you.

But this doesn't happen without openness and vulnerability, which is one of the hallmarks of biblical friendship. When David writes, "The friendship of the LORD is for those who fear him" (Ps. 25:14), the Hebrew word for friendship can also mean "secret" (hence the ESV footnote "secret counsel"). Friendship is connected to secrecy. A friend is someone you tell your secrets to, someone you let in on the real things that are going on in your life. They're the ones who really know what's going on with you. They know your temptations, and they know what most delights your heart. They know how to pray for you instinctively.

This is true intimacy. In our world, being deeply known and deeply loved often feel like alternatives. We worry that if someone really knew us, they might not love us as much. So as Tim Keller has said, we become our own public-relations managers. We cultivate the sort of image we want the world to have of us. We deftly keep hidden what we don't ever want people to find out about us. It is the character of much of life in this world and has been ever since Adam and Eve felt the need to start covering up around each other. There's something vulnerable about being deeply known. So when we do find people we can share our inner selves with, it is a huge relief and a great gift.

This view of friendship is reinforced by Jesus himself. In a startling passage Jesus describes his followers as friends:

> No longer do I call you servants, for the servant does not know what his master is doing; but I have called you friends, for all that I have heard from my Father I have made known to you. (John 15:15)

Notice Jesus's reasoning. Jesus is telling us what he considers real friendship to consist of. A master-servant relationship, much like a boss-employee relationship in our own day, is primarily functional: one sets the work to be done, and the other goes off and does it. In neither instance is the boss or master under any obligation to explain himself fully or to open up about what is really on his heart or mind—"the servant does not know what his master is doing."

But a friend *does* open up. This is Jesus's point.

Yes, he is the leader and his disciples are to follow him. But we will miss something vital if we leave it just like that. He is our master, our Lord; but he is not *just* that to us. Jesus says that, unlike the servant or subordinate, we *do* know what he is doing. And, remarkably, he has not just opened up an itty-bitty amount but *completely* to us. All that he has to share with us from the Father, he has shared. He's not holding back vital things from us. There's no need-to-know dynamic or hierarchy of clearance. As far as he's concerned, what he knows, we now know. He has let us in entirely. It is beautiful. He is the friend par excellence.

By its very nature friendship is a wonderful form of intimacy. The friend is the person who knows you at your sparkling best and shameful worst and yet still loves you. To be so deeply known and so deeply loved is precious.

This is what we all need. Proverbs commends friendship not because it is a nice bonus in life, but because it is key to living wisely in God's world.

> A man of many companions may come to ruin,
>> but there is a friend who sticks closer than a brother.
>> (Prov. 18:24)

This proverb does more than just set friendship apart from family or loose companionship. There's a closeness, an intimacy, to friendship without which we become vulnerable to ruin. Proverbs has so much to say about friendship, precisely because it is a key component of wisdom.

So it matters to all of us. I've spoken a number of times on this issue in church contexts and more than once have had the sense that many of the married people were thinking to themselves, *It's so good for the singles to hear teaching on this*. But the fact is, all of us need friends—married people every bit as much as singles. I've seen more than one marriage run into difficulty because the couple had looked entirely to each other to meet all their friendship and intimacy needs and had not pursued good friendships alongside their marriage. It's not always easy to foster close friendships when you're established as a family, but it's a vital discipline to open up family life to others around you.

When we find we're able to cultivate these Proverbs-type friendships, we find it's possible to enjoy a huge amount of intimacy in life. It is deep intimacy any of us can enjoy and yet many around us never experience (sadly even sometimes within marriage).

As a single person, there is a depth of intimacy my married friends enjoy that I am not able to experience—to share pretty much all of life with one other person. But it is not as simple to say that I have less intimacy in my life as a result. Singleness gives me a capacity for a range of friendships I wouldn't be able to sustain if I was married. I have close friends ranging from twenty years younger than I to twenty years older, covering a geographical and cultural range.

A more flexible lifestyle makes it possible to see them in a way I couldn't imagine if I had my own family to look after. Some time ago, a couple I am close to called me to say they'd just had some sudden bad news from their doctor and were clearly very distressed. Being single made it relatively easy for me to drop everything, throw a toothbrush in an overnight bag, jump in the car, and go visit them. It meant a lot to me to be able to do that. Another couple I know lost a child to suicide. I was able to stay with them for a few days. It was a sad privilege to be with them in a time of such deep trauma.

Singleness lends itself to this kind of intimacy; it provides the opportunity and freedom for it. So while I might not know the unique depth of intimacy a married friend enjoys, there is a unique *breadth* of intimacy available to singles that married friends would not be as able to experience.

4

Singleness Means No Family

Some time ago I randomly met someone I hadn't seen for about ten years. As we caught up on a decade's worth of news, I asked about her kids. When I'd known her before, she'd had two teenagers, who were now in their late twenties, so I asked what they were up to.

"One of them is married, and the other is engaged. So they're both sorted."

I was glad to hear they were doing well. But my mind stuck on that last word—*sorted*.

I guess I know what she meant. But it was hard to avoid the implication. What did that say about me? Am I *unsorted*?

Comments like this, often unintentionally, tend to imply that we singles are a little like loose threads that have been left dangling and need to be tied up. It's like we're still awaiting processing. Once people have become established in their own family unit, they're good to go. They're ready for life. Or—as my friend put it—sorted.

There are a couple of problems with this. One is thinking that having your own family unit means you've now somehow future-proofed the rest of your life. But we know that's not the case. I've already mentioned examples of some of the "worldly troubles" married people can face.

But the other problem (and the focus of this chapter) is the assumption that being single means you don't have family. As we saw in the previous chapter, the Bible speaks of friendship as a wonderfully intimate way of relating to others. But it is not the only nonsexual means of enjoying intimacy. It is common for people to assume singleness means closing the door on having family. But, again, this need not be the case. Just as the Bible has a different conception of friendship, it also has a very different way of helping us think about family.

How Jesus Reconstitutes Family

We see this reflected throughout the New Testament. Jesus suggests it even early on in his ministry. Someone brings up the matter of Jesus's physical family—his mother and half-brothers.

> He answered them, "Who are my mother and my brothers?"
> And looking about at those who sat around him, he said,
> "Here are my mother and my brothers! For whoever does
> the will of God, he is my brother and sister and mother."
> (Mark 3:33–35)

Jesus reconfigures how we are to think about family. His real family is defined along spiritual rather than biological lines. We become part of his family when we follow the will of God. It is our spiritual orientation rather than our physical birth that now becomes ultimately defining.

This is foundational to what the New Testament goes on to say about family as the people of God. It means, if we're Christians, that if we have the privilege of belonging to a physical family, we mustn't think it is our *only* family. And if we don't have any physical family, we're not to think we have been left with no experience of family life at all. Actually, Jesus says this should not be the case. Quite the opposite, in fact.

How Jesus Promises Family

Take a look at one of Jesus's most remarkable but lesser-known promises:

> Peter began to say to him, "See, we have left everything and followed you."
>
> Jesus said, "Truly, I say to you, there is no one who has left house or brothers or sisters or mother or father or children or lands, for my sake and for the gospel, who will not receive a hundredfold now in this time, houses and brothers and sisters and mothers and children and lands, with persecutions, and in the age to come eternal life." (Mark 10:28–30)

In this passage we have just had the well-known encounter between Jesus and the rich young man. He bounded up to Jesus, seemingly full of enthusiasm for getting on board the Jesus train but was not willing to leave behind what Jesus required him to. And so he left the encounter sorrowful. It is all very poignant.

But Peter immediately senses an opportunity to be Peter and jumps in with, "See, we have left everything and followed you." Now we can't hear the tone of Peter's voice, so we need to be careful in trying to ascertain his motives. It is entirely possible, for example, that he is speaking out of despair: "Jesus, you do know we actually *left* things to follow you, right? You know we all had careers and stuff going on back home, right?" But given what we see elsewhere in the Gospel accounts of

Peter's impetuousness and capacity for casting himself as the spiritual hero, he's almost certainly bragging in this verse. A promising would-be follower has just failed discipleship 101, so Peter reminds Jesus of who his star pupils are: "Jesus," says Peter, eyes gazing at the far horizon in case anyone's Instagramming any of this, "We were willing to lay it all down for you. *Everything.*" He's already imagining the museum someone will one day open, commemorating this staggering display of discipleship.

Either way, Jesus's response is stunning when we stop to think about it. The trouble is, we often don't. Because this little section comes hot on the heels of such a famous encounter, it is often skipped over in Bible notes and sermons. By the time the preacher is done explaining the science of why a camel can't pass through the eye of a needle (even if you stick it in a blender first), there's no time to go into this quick back-and-forth between Jesus and Peter. But notice some key things.

First, Jesus assumes people will leave things to follow him. It is basic discipleship. It is what he has always said. I love this about Jesus: he never buries things in the small print. Jesus is front and center about the cost of following him. Discipleship is wonderful, but it's not meant to be easy. Jesus isn't sensitive to good marketing; he just says it like it is.

Second, Jesus assumes the most costly things to leave will be relational and familial, having to leave behind certain patterns of intimacy or our whole family and kin. For some disciples this is literally the case. People from some backgrounds know that the moment they follow Jesus, they will be forever shunned by their families. Imagine that. Never again being able to see your brothers and sisters. Never really knowing what your nieces and nephews grew up to be like. Not seeing your parents and relatives or the home and land you grew up in. Jesus's words are not metaphorical but literal for so many of those who follow him. Discipleship is costly. Sometimes it's *really* costly.

But, third, notice how Jesus responds to all this. He doesn't tell them to just grit their teeth and wait for the age to come when it will finally be worth it. No. Jesus shows them it will be worth it *even in this life*. Whatever someone might have to leave behind to follow him, he will replace, in godly kind and far greater measure. Even those who leave whole family networks behind for the sake of Jesus will receive back from him vastly more—a hundredfold.

If I can put it this way, this is the *true* prosperity gospel. Jesus doesn't promise us greater wealth and prosperity if we follow him. He doesn't promise a glowing property portfolio if we go all in with him. He doesn't say that for every dollar you give him, he'll give you back a hundred. No. Just as the cost is cast in relational, familial terms, so too is the blessing. Jesus promises us family—"houses and brothers and sisters and mothers and children and lands."[1] (And, yes, a side order of persecutions too, whether we ordered it or not. That just comes as part of the bundle.)

It is an extraordinary promise. Whatever relational cost our discipleship may incur, however much family we may lose in the course of following Christ, Jesus is saying that even in this life it will be worth it. Following him means an abundance of spiritual family. Nature may have given us only one mother and one father; the gospel gives us far more.

Remarkable though they are, Jesus's words are really an expansion of what God had always promised to do. In fact, it's who he is, as Psalms reminds us: "God sets the lonely in families" (Ps. 68:6 NIV).

It's easy to read a verse like that and think, "Aw. It's so nice that God does that." But the fact is, it's actually deeply challenging, because we're the families of Psalm 68 in which God is placing the lonely. We are the mothers and fathers, sisters and brothers, and sons and daughters that Jesus is promising in Mark 10. It makes Jesus's promise quite unusual: there's a sense in which it depends on us to fulfill it. Those who would otherwise be alone are grafted into the community life of his people. When God draws people to himself, he draws them to one another as well. The people of Jesus Christ are to be family.

We see this reflected throughout the New Testament, where the church is repeatedly spoken of as a family. One of the apostle Paul's favorite terms for the local church is "the household of God":

> So then you are no longer strangers and aliens, but you are fellow citizens with the saints and members of the household of God. (Eph. 2:19)

> I hope to come to you soon, but I am writing these things to you so that, if I delay, you may know how one ought to behave in the household of God, which is the church of the living God. (1 Tim. 3:14–15)

There is not meant to be anything nominal about this way of speaking. It is common to use this language of family in church circles—calling one another "brothers and sisters"—without really thinking about it. But it is not meant to be honorary. Nor is it "just a bit of good PR"[2] to make our churches sound friendly. It is real and meant to be lived out as such.

Paul gives us an example of what this can mean in practice. Writing to Timothy, a younger pastor, Paul says:

> Do not rebuke an older man but encourage him as you would
> a father, younger men as brothers, older women as mothers,
> younger women as sisters, in all purity. (1 Tim. 5:1–2)

This is revealing. Timothy is to look at the people in his church as family and treat them accordingly. But there is more than that. He is not just to treat them as family but as *close* family. Paul doesn't say, "Treat older men as great-uncles, or, "younger men as distant cousins." They're not distant family, but immediate family.

This changes everything. Distant family we can get away with seeing only irregularly, maybe once a year or two at a big gathering. You sense the connection, and it means something, but there is no deep investment in the other person. But immediate family implies a much tighter connection. We are to be there for one another and lean on one another. We have a stake in one another. What happens to one affects all of us.

This has some significant implications for how we think about family in general. We may well have been blessed by our biological, nuclear family. Maybe you're married, and maybe you have children. This is a precious gift and one that you have solemn responsibilities toward. But it is not your only kind of family, or the only set of people to whom you owe such a significant amount. If you're a Christian, the fellowship to which you belong is your family too. And while that might feel like it creates a tension or competition, the opposite is actually meant to be the case. These two types of family are designed to be overlapping and interlocking in a way that helps each to flourish in a way that wouldn't otherwise be the case.

In my part of the world (southern England), just as in many other relatively prosperous parts of the West, the assumption is that nuclear families are the basic unit in which we are meant to do life. With one, you're sorted; without one—well, you kinda need one. And because this is the case, many people simply assume these family units are meant to be self-contained and self-sufficient. The aspiration is to have a wife or a husband, 2.5 children, a black Labrador, and a nice house. Once all this is acquired, you have what you need for doing life, so you then pull up the drawbridge and live happily ever after.

A sign of this is the way we increasingly esteem privacy. The wealthier we become, the more we physically demarcate and separate our family unit from the rest of the world. The drawbridge, meant metaphorically, becomes as literal as we can afford it to be. We want our family life to be sequestered. This attitude all too easily spills into the church as well.

But the self-sufficient nuclear family is not a concept we see in the Bible. Instead, we see that our spiritual family needs our biological family, and our biological family needs our spiritual family. If church is our family, then the boundary of our physical family life should be porous and flexible rather than fixed and inviolable.

It is easy to see how this can help those of us who are single. It can be a great blessing to be involved in the physical family life of others.

I've seen this to be true for myself in so many ways. There are some families I am particularly close to. One or two of these, with younger kids, will frequently ask if I'd like to be involved in the bedtime routine, anything from brushing the children's teeth to reading them a bedtime story and praying with them. It's great fun. A friend's little daughter often asks me to do this whether I've volunteered or not. Now, not every single person is the same as I. Some will find rolling up their sleeves and getting stuck into the rhythms of someone else's family only serves to remind them that they don't have one of their own. But it's a slice of family life I enjoy being part of.

Another family I spend a lot of time with was recently heading into what they knew would be a particularly crazy week, so I offered to help out and do the school run for them for a few days. I figured it would be one less thing for them to have to organize.

"We couldn't ask you to do that!"

"You didn't—I offered," I replied.

For them it is a daily chore. But for me it is a novelty to do this for a few days. I never get to do a school run. What parents often find part of the mundane grind of daily life, some of us singles might actually enjoy. Plus it's a great way to chat with their kids and find out what their school life is like. I find out who their friends are and what classes they most love and hate (and get to pick up the latest colloquialisms). I know how to pray for them a whole ton better after even a short journey in a car.

Other times I might come around and cook for everyone. Much as I love having people over, sometimes it's way more practical for me to bring the cooking to the family than to get all of them to my place at the same time. It is a way to hang out together without much disruption to them.

Things like this make a family feel inclusive. They're not just having you around; they're opening up their family life to you and letting you join in. Andrea Trevenna describes another way in which families can reflect this more porous view of family life:

> I love it when I go round to married friends' homes and see not only (or even) their wedding photos, pictures of their children and whole-family holiday snaps, but also photos of other families and friends (sometimes including me!). This reminds me that "family" doesn't just mean the nuclear

family, that I am not on my own, and that as a Christian I am part of a wonderful wider family.[3]

This might sound a little weird, but I feel reassured when families feel able to have arguments around me. It doesn't mean it's necessarily fun to be there when it's happening, but it confirms that they see me as part of normal life. None of them is putting on any special behavior when I am around. Sometimes it's actually *not* making a fuss over a visitor that can make them feel more special and at home. They're not being given a specially vetted version of family life; they're being included in the real deal, warts and all.

This also serves, of course, to help singles realize that family life is not idyllic. There are certainly times when all the kids are being cute and precocious. But at other times there is open warfare. It is the same with marriages. I've seen enough marriages sufficiently to know that it is not all a stroll in the park. Couples do not live "happily ever after" once they've said their vows. It helps singles to see a realistic image of what life is often like on the other side of the fence.

This is the difference between what the Bible means by hospitality and what often passes for it in Western culture. Too often what we're really doing is not hospitality but entertaining. We're putting on a good show. We're showing someone the Instagram version of our home life rather than the actual version of it. A sign that this is the case is that hospitality becomes infrequent and extravagant. But in the Bible, hospitality is opening up our real lives to others (often and especially the stranger) and inviting them in. You don't technically need a physical space to invite people into (which in crowded cities is something many increasingly can't afford). It is as much about doing life with others, wherever and however we happen to do it.

This is something all of us are called to do. Some will have a particular ministry in this area, but it is required of all believers:

> Rejoice in hope, be patient in tribulation, be constant in prayer. Contribute to the needs of the saints and seek to show hospitality. (Rom. 12:12–13)

Hospitality clearly matters. Paul puts it up there with praying and helping the poor as an obligation for all Christians. Peter says much the same thing:

> Show hospitality to one another without grumbling. (1 Pet. 4:9)

Peter not only reminds us we need to do it but that we're not to do it begrudgingly. We're to do it gladly. Peter is not so much telling us to do a certain *kind of thing* but to be a certain *kind of person*: someone who is willing and eager to share life and home with others. It is even important enough to be a qualification for anyone in church leadership:

> An overseer must be above reproach, the husband of one wife, sober-minded, self-controlled, respectable, hospitable, able to teach, not a drunkard, not violent but gentle, not quarrelsome, not a lover of money. (1 Tim. 3:2–3)

I have seen people disqualified from church leadership because of drunkenness and marital infidelity, but I've never heard of hospitality even being considered in a would-be pastor. Yet Paul lists it alongside these other failings as being just as much a deal breaker.

By calling us to show hospitality, the New Testament is not requiring us to add yet more to our already overloaded schedules but to think of ways to fold others into what we are already doing. The impact of this can be huge:

> Do not neglect to show hospitality to strangers, for thereby some have entertained angels unawares. (Heb. 13:2)

This is a reference to some events in the life of Abraham, when he took in some strangers without realizing they were actually the Lord and his angels (Gen. 18:1–8). The general point the writer of Hebrews is making is that hospitality is something that God can use in all sorts of ways we never would have expected. We must never underestimate what can be achieved for the kingdom of God around the kitchen table. It is a place God loves to use.

The importance and impact of hospitality should not surprise us. There is nothing arbitrary about the fact that this is required of Christians, or that God loves to use it so powerfully. When we think about it, hospitality is a profound expression of what the gospel is. It reflects exactly what God has done for us. Look at how Paul describes the work of Christ:

> Remember that you were . . . separated from Christ, alienated from the commonwealth of Israel and strangers to the covenants of promise. . . . But now in Christ Jesus you who once were far off have been brought near by the blood of Christ. (Eph. 2:12–13)

In other words, we have all been saved by divine hospitality. We were far away from God but have now been brought into his presence, into his very household. God has taken us in and seated us at his table. And he has done all this through the blood of Christ. He was forsaken and left out so that we could be folded in. The sign that we have received this kind of hospitality is that we offer it to others.

It is easy for singles to sometimes think that all the initiative must lie with the families, and certainly it is often easier for a family to extend a meal by an extra portion than for a single to cook for an additional four or five, but that is no reason for any of us to sit around waiting for families to do all the reaching out. We need to find ways of getting alongside and taking initiative too.

But for those of us who do have our own physical family, it is worth asking who we regularly include in our family life, who we're opening ourselves to. If we have a spare room, are we using that to be a home to others? Not all families will be able to open up to the same extent and in the same way, but I suspect many of us could be doing more, maybe much more, than we are.

Look again at the "hundredfold" blessing Jesus is promising:

Truly, I say to you, there is no one who has left house or brothers or sisters or mother or father or children or lands, for my sake and for the gospel, who will not receive a hundredfold now in this time, houses and brothers and sisters and mothers and children and lands, with persecutions, and in the age to come eternal life. (Mark 10:29–30)

Think about the "houses" and "fields" Jesus is talking about. He is not promising his followers an expansive property portfolio. He is not talking about real estate but about something much more precious: homes that are being shared. Just as we are the mothers and fathers, brothers and sisters, and sons and daughters he is promising to those who lack them, so also we are to provide houses and fields.

So ponder this question for a moment or two: Other than a neighbor in case of an emergency, who else has a key to your home? In other words: is there anyone apart from those who have your surname whom you truly regard as family? Anyone who is family enough that they have the freedom to come around any time, without an invitation or even advance notice, just as your own blood family does?

A couple I know very well recently did just this for me—they gave me a key to their apartment. "This is yours now—you're family." They didn't mean it to be a grand moment; they just tossed a key in my direction. But it felt significant. I was incredibly touched. And it is not the first time someone has done this for me.

Much of this book has been written at a desk that's become a regular workplace in a friend's house a few hours from where I live. It has become a second home. It is a wonderful place. From the moment I arrive to the moment I leave, the dog doesn't leave my side but faithfully accompanies me from room to room. The cats clock where I am and eventually, and often silently, park themselves nearby too. One of them decides I've done enough work for the time being and sprawls herself across my laptop so that my fingers are freed from the keyboard to pet her. Once the dog realizes play is on offer, he jumps to his feet, tail thumping against everything in range (including the cats), and we all go exploring in the woods outside for a few minutes.

The animal affection alone is lovely to bask in, but it is the family here that makes it feel like home. We've been close for many years now, and have gone through deep tragedy and wonderful joy together. Soon after they moved here, they not only invited me to visit but said they wanted me to leave some clothes and toiletries in one of the closets so I wouldn't need to pack for future visits. So although I don't own a single square meter of real estate anywhere in the world, it turns out I have many homes and fields.

As my friend Rosaria Butterfield puts it, "the gospel comes with a house key."[4]

I also have sons and daughters, in a certain kind of way.

I was just staying with another family I know well. It was the start of the new school year for kids, and the evening before the first day back, the local elementary school had an open evening so that families could come in with their kids and meet the teachers and break the ice again after a long summer break. My friend's eleven-year-old twin boys insisted I come too as they wanted to show me their school. One of them was feeling a little apprehensive about starting back at school, so I was keen to do anything that might help. But it turned out the twins didn't just want me to see where they went to school; they wanted each of their teachers to meet their English friend. It was very touching.

Some of this might sound as if the benefit is only one way. But in reality it is a win-win. Last year I gave a talk on some of this to a group of pastors in another region of the country. A day or so later, someone I barely know wrote to me. He wasn't at the meeting and isn't a pastor, but he wanted to thank me for what I said. He is a single man, and one of the pastors at the meeting was a friend of his and had just given him a house key. Then a few months later someone came up to me and said he'd been at that same talk I'd given. It turned out he was the pastor who had given out that house key. He wanted to thank me for the challenge, because it had been such a blessing since then to have this friend more involved in his family's life.

The fact is, it is good for the families themselves to have others folded into their life. Such inclusion helps not just the people you include but the family as well. This is the way God designed it to be: the physical and spiritual families we belong to need each other. It's not just that others need your biological family; your biological family needs them too. The boundary of your family life needs to be porous for your family's own good.

This is worked out on many levels. A mother once told me how much she loved spending time with singles at church. It's too easy, she said, to surround herself only with other mothers whose kids are at a similar stage to her own. While there's value in sharing the similarities—they can compare notes and encourage one another—the danger is that parenting can absorb the whole of the parent's life and identity. This mother said that meeting with singles reminded her that life is going on out there beyond the realms of childcare. Catching up with the singles she knows gives her a lifeline to the wider world she senses she could easily lose contact with.

I think too of the opportunities I have as a single man to encourage my friends who are married (which is the vast majority of them). One way I can use my singleness is to commit to praying for them as husbands. I don't have personal experience of marriage to offer them, but I know enough of what Scripture says to know what they should be aiming for as husbands and to know how much they'll need support and accountability to get there.

But the involvement of others in family life can particularly help children. I can still remember the first time I was asked to be a godfather. I was only in my early twenties, and a slightly older couple with whom I'd become good friends were bracing themselves for the arrival of their second child. They asked me to be the godfather. What struck me was the reason. They said it wasn't about birthdays and presents (which is just as well; if her age corresponded to the number of birthdays I've remembered, she'd be the only toddler with a driver's license). Instead, they said, "We need you to pray for us as parents. And we also want you to be someone she can talk to when she's older and doesn't feel she can talk to us."

They assumed that there'd be times in their daughter's life when they might not be the best people for her to talk to. I thought that was very wise. The fact is that no two parents can be everything their children need them to be. Stating this reality should not be controversial, but I often feel congregations bristle when I say it. It should be obvious. All parents are limited, and all parents are sinful. They can't possibly hope to be the best at everything their kids are going to need. Once again we see the myth of the self-sufficient family at work. Parents can have the unrealistic idea that their children are flawless. (As someone once put it, those who call their baby an "angel" clearly don't understand babies *or* angels.)

Parents can also have an unrealistic idea about what their parenting can achieve. Every parent has areas of natural capability and areas of natural weakness. None of us is a full and complete human being in ourselves. So every parent has blind spots. A child who gets her primary spiritual input only from her parents will only really grasp a somewhat incomplete or skewed version of the Christian life. No parents are going to get every aspect of it right, so kids having the input of other people in the wider church family is not a luxury but a necessity. Hopefully this is a role youth and children's leaders naturally take at church. But it is good to have family friends involved in the spiritual formation of children too. Kids can then see in the details of how others live that this Christianity stuff is not just what their parents think, and that other people follow Jesus too. And because each couple and each family have their own eccentricities, the input of other honorary aunts and uncles can have a moderating effect. As Ray Ortlund observes, "Our various family backgrounds left every one of us at least a little weird."⁵ It takes humility to realize it, but your children stand a much better chance of becoming well-rounded if it's not just you they look to in life.

It is also one of the ways we see Jesus's promise in Mark 10 of disciples being given children as a result of following him. As I've said, it's a wonderful privilege to be involved in the family life of some of my friends. To be given any kind of spiritual role in the lives of children is an enormous responsibility. Parents need to be careful in thinking about who has this kind of input. In this day and age especially, we are all too conscious of the danger of the wrong people being involved in our family life. Our children are vulnerable. It is good to be mindful of this and discerning about whose input we allow them. But while it is a significant danger, it is not the only one. While having the wrong sort of input is a justifiable concern, so too is having no other input at all.

In a couple of weeks I will go on vacation, and I can't wait. It's not because I've been busy and am looking forward to a break (though I have been, and I am). Nor is it because I'm going anywhere glamorous and exotic. People make jokes about the place I plan to vacation. Many of them live there. I don't need shots to be allowed admittance, and there's no risk of running into celebrities. I'm going to one of the least glamorous parts of the UK. No, what I'm most excited about is who I'm going there with. Every year a gang of about fifteen of us go away together for a week. The group has been doing this for about fifteen years now, with the occasional addition and subtraction over the years. We're normally comprised of two families, with six kids between them, aged five to fifteen, and three or four singles.

All of us love it. We're a large group, so we don't have to do everything together. If someone wants time alone, he or she can easily slope off without feeling antisocial. What the younger kids are into is not necessarily what the rest of us want to do. A couple of the guys are steam train enthusiasts and, for some reason, need to spend at least a day of their vacation riding on the sort of steam engines the rest of the world happily evolved away from several generations ago. (Admission: we all secretly love it.) There'll be a day or so at the beach, and another just hanging out at the house.

What makes it work is that it is a win-win. The parents love it, as it gives them a bit of a break from cooking for a whole family each day and peers to catch up with. Kids love it because there is no shortage of people to hang out and play with. And singles like me love it, as it gives us an excuse to do the sort of things we can only really get away with if there are kids around, like digging sandcastles or defenses against the incoming tide. It's one of my favorite weeks of the year. It's a family holiday, regardless of whether or not we technically have a family.

How Jesus Provides Family

Some time ago I was planning a sermon series on Paul's letter to Titus. The first sermon covered just the first four verses, where Paul introduces himself and greets his recipient. It's the part of New Testament letters we tend to skip over on our way to the main content, so I thought it would be interesting to pause and give a whole message on what Paul had to say about himself and his friend Titus. Stopping and noticing the detail of even familiar Scriptures is where I often find myself learning significant lessons.

Take how Paul describes himself:

Paul, a servant of God and an apostle of Jesus Christ. (Titus 1:1)

81

Not unusual in terms of what Paul normally says about himself but radical when we stop and think about it. "Servant" (as my Bible's footnote points out) really means "slave." "Apostle" is someone especially authorized by Jesus to speak and write on his behalf. What's interesting is how easily, for Paul, servitude and authority go together. It is a distinctively Christian way of thinking. Some of us are parents or bosses or group leaders at church or are just the natural ringleaders that others tend to follow. But if we're Christians, it means we are to use that authority exclusively and maximally for the sake of others. That is the template given to us in Christ, who expressed absolute authority through absolute servitude. It is what has now gripped his apostle and is to so grip us that we treat any natural position we're given in life as a means of spending ourselves for the good of others rather than ourselves.

That one verse alone gave me a huge amount to think about. But it was what Paul said about Titus that I found even more striking:

To Titus, my true child in a common faith. (Titus 1:4)

Again, Paul compresses big truth into the space of few words. (Paul would have been great on Twitter.) Were it not for the fact that I had to get half a sermon out of these words I probably wouldn't have looked at them so closely. But they've truly become life changing. Paul describes Titus not as "my dear workmate and colleague" or even as "my dear friend." He calls him "my true child."

This challenges how we typically think of Paul. We tend to think of how he was single, never married, and didn't have kids. But that's not entirely true. Paul *was* single. He wasn't married. But he *did* have children. Titus is his "true child."

And this is not some first-century equivalent of saying, "Hey, kiddo." Paul literally describes Titus as his *legitimate begotten*. This is not airy-fairy language to make Paul feel better about himself as a single. It is real. Paul had led Titus to faith in Christ. Something generative happened as a result of Paul's ministry to him. Titus was not only a fellow believer with Paul or a fellow brother in Christ. He had become, spiritually, Paul's begotten.

There are times when singleness is hard. One of those times can be when you reach the age where virtually all your friends have kids and you don't. (This can be painful for childless couples too, of course.) It hit me a few years ago at a good friend's wedding. I was watching the father of the bride dancing with his daughter. Her sister told me he'd taken some dance lessons especially for this. He wanted to be able to share this moment with his girl, a final fatherly moment before she started a new home and new family life with her husband. It was lovely to see. But painful too. I realized I would never have a daughter to dance with on her wedding day. I don't know why that suddenly hit me—the idea had never occurred to me before. But there it was, and it cut me up deeply.

Another single friend mentioned to me that, for her, it was the time she spent with a friend looking at this friend's pictures of a daughter's graduation. That was what suddenly hit her—never celebrating the graduation of her own child. It might be any number of things for each one of us. A sudden, unexpected moment of bereavement. So a verse like this one in Titus is an amazing encouragement. There is a kind of parenthood available to us even as unmarried singles. Titus is Paul's begotten.

And, as it turns out, Titus was not an only child. Paul did a lot of begetting. Look at what he had to say about Timothy:

Timothy, my true child in the faith. (1 Tim. 1:2)

Timothy, my beloved child. (2 Tim. 1:2)

You then, my child. (2 Tim 2:1)

Timothy, my beloved and faithful child in the Lord. (1 Cor. 4:17)

Paul could even become a spiritual father while in prison. He writes to Philemon, "I appeal to you for my child, Onesimus, whose father I became in my imprisonment" (Philem. 10). In fact, so widespread was Paul in his spiritual begetting that even whole churches were fathered by him:

> For though you have countless guides in Christ, you do not have many fathers. For I became your father in Christ Jesus through the gospel. (1 Cor. 4:15)

> My little children, for whom I am again in the anguish of childbirth until Christ is formed in you. (Gal. 4:19)

But it would be a mistake to think of this as some kind of sappy consolation prize for those who miss the real thing. Titus is Paul's real son, "my true son." Not a sort of, kinda like, or equivalent of, but *legitimate*.

None of this is out of the blue. The trajectory of Scripture has been pointing this way for a long time. Long ago God told his people that there is a blessing available to the childless even greater than that of physical children:

> For thus says the LORD:
> "To the eunuchs who keep my Sabbaths,
>   who choose the things that please me
>   and hold fast my covenant,

> I will give in my house and within my walls
> > a monument and a name
> > better than sons and daughters;
> I will give them an everlasting name
> > that shall not be cut off. (Isa. 56:4–5)

This perspective explains Jesus's intriguing response to a woman who yelled out from a crowd about how blessed Mary was to be his mother:

> As he said these things, a woman in the crowd raised her voice and said to him, "Blessed is the womb that bore you, and the breasts at which you nursed!" But he said, "Blessed rather are those who hear the word of God and keep it!" (Luke 11:27–28)

Children are a great blessing. The Bible underlines that repeatedly. Children are a responsibility, for sure, but they are also a great gift from God.

But if any parent had cause to be called "blessed," it's Mary. She had all the regular joys of motherhood—a bouncing baby, the thrill of the first tooth and the first step. But hers was also a unique blessing. Her boy was no less than the eternal Son of God. The One who filled her womb and then fed at her breasts was God himself. You can just imagine Mary's Christmas family newsletter wiping the floor with everyone else's. So no wonder this nameless woman in the crowd calls out to Jesus in this way. Mary was blessed.

She was. Uniquely so. But what brought Mary greatest blessing is something that any of us can share with her. Jesus says there's a blessing greater than that of a parent, even than that of being a parent to the Son of God. And that is to be an obedient Christian. If you hear the Word of God and keep it, you are more blessed than any parent of any child. But there is more.

If the blessing of physical sons and daughters is not itself the greatest blessing, then it's also the case that physical children are not the only—or even the greatest—kind of children we can have. Men and women produce physical children. But the gospel itself also produces offspring. We see this in how Isaiah foretells the death of Jesus:

> It was the will of the LORD to crush him;
>   he has put him to grief;
> when his soul makes an offering for guilt,
>   he shall see his offspring. (Isa. 53:10)

Commenting on these words John Piper writes,

> When the Messiah dies as "an offering for guilt" and rises again to "prolong his days" forever, he will by that great saving act produce many children: He will "see his offspring." In other words, the new people of God formed by the Messiah will not be formed by physical procreation but by the atoning death of Christ.[6]

The result of this is that those who mourn at not being able to physically reproduce can know the blessing of being involved in producing spiritual offspring. As Piper goes on to say, "Single people in Christ have zero disadvantage in bearing children for God and may, in some ways, have a great advantage."[7] Hence Paul's language about Titus and others being his begotten.

Isaiah shows us a further distinction between physical and spiritual progeny:

> "Sing, O barren one, who did not bear;
>   break forth into singing and cry aloud,

you who have not been in labor!
For the children of the desolate one will be more
than the children of her who is married," says the
LORD. (Isa. 54:1)

Not only will the barren lady be able to rejoice at being able to have children; those children will in some way be "more" than those of normal physical birth. This relates not only to the multitudes we can father in Christ (as Paul did), but also to the extent of the legacy such spiritual parenting produces. Barry Danylak concludes:

> Like Isaiah's barren woman, Paul's legacy was greater than that of any physical parents', for Paul's progeny were those begotten in Christ through the limitless power of the gospel for an eternal inheritance in heaven.[8]

Blood, they say, is thicker than water. But the blood of Jesus is thicker still. Better than a lifelong legacy is an eternal one.

This opens up the prospect of parenting to all who are single in Christ. Regardless of our marital status we can be involved in bringing forth the spiritual offspring of the gospel. So it is that John Piper can say:

> Paul was a great father and never married. And does he not speak beautifully for single women in Christ in 1 Thessalonians 2:7 when he writes, "We were gentle among you, like a nursing mother taking care of her own children"? So it will be said of many single women in Christ, "She was a great mother and never married."[9]

We see a wonderful example of this in C. S. Lewis's classic story *The Great Divorce*. The narrator is taken by a guide around heaven and at one point sees an enormous procession.

There is a line each of boys and girls; he sees musicians, dancing, celebration, and even giant angels. At the center of it all, and in whose honor it is all taking place, he sees a beautiful lady. She is, the guide explains, someone of significant greatness. On earth she was unheard of, a woman called Sarah Smith who never had any biological children. But in heaven she is "one of the great ones," and the large number of young men and women flanking her are, in fact, her sons and daughters. The guide explains:

> Every young man or boy that met her became her son—even if it was only the boy who brought the meat to her back door. Every girl that met her was her daughter. . . . Her motherhood was of a different kind. Those on whom it fell went back to their natural parents loving them more.[10]

Sarah Smith didn't have any biological children on earth but was a spiritual mother to many.

The greatest example of this kind of spiritual parenting is, of course, Jesus himself. Writer Bethany Jenkins comments:

> As a Christian, I worship a man who was a biologically childless parent. Jesus Christ never married, never had kids, yet he said: "Behold, I and the children God has given me" (Heb. 2:13). And consider what the prophet says of him: "When his soul makes an offering for guilt, he shall see his offspring. . . . Out of the anguish of his soul he shall see and be satisfied" (Isa. 53:10–11). Jesus never held a son or daughter in his arms, but he nonetheless came to bear children, to give birth to a people—like me and perhaps you—who now bear his family resemblance.[11]

In a recent series of tweets, Matthew Lee Anderson concluded that the church needs to think more expansively about the whole concept of parenthood:

> Within the community of the church . . . "parenthood" is a
> vocation open to all, including singles and the infertile. It is
> an ecclesiastically centered way of cultivating maternal and
> paternal love in its deepest orientation, namely, toward the
> kingdom. If this is true, then there are aspects of parenthood
> that are disclosed to single and infertile people. It is not a
> realm closed to them.[12]

This helps to answer an important concern sometimes raised
about singleness in the church, that it somehow represents a
neglect of the responsibility given to humanity at the start of
the Bible.

In the biblical account of creation, as soon as God creates
humanity he commissions them to do the work for which he
has created them:

> God blessed them. And God said to them, "Be fruitful and
> multiply and fill the earth and subdue it, and have dominion
> over the fish of the sea and over the birds of the heavens and
> over every living thing that moves on the earth." (Gen. 1:28)

These newly minted image bearers were given clear instructions
about their new home. They were to have dominion over it, later
unpacked in Genesis 2:15 as "to work it and keep it"—to develop it and care for it. And they were to fill it—to "be fruitful
and multiply." These image bearers were to cover the planet
with this image. The whole earth needs the human touch. It's a
big world, and at that point there were only two people. Lots of
multiplying needed to happen.

It's commonly called the "creation mandate," humanity's
responsibility to the world in which we've been placed. It represents our collective vocation from God. This is what we've
been made to do. All of us. It's a big deal. Little wonder that

doing constructive work (paid or unpaid) and starting families instinctively mean so much to us. We're all meant to be rolling up our sleeves and doing what we can to contribute to the ongoing flourishing of our species.

So singleness can easily appear to be a bit of an obstacle to all this. Those of us who will only ever be single will not be taking part in the multiplication God has called us to do. I'm on track to remain unmarried and childless. My little branch of the family tree is not going to continue through me. I will be a genealogical dead-end. A genetic cul-de-sac. I will be contributing no more Allberrys to the world.

Little wonder, then, that we singles can be thought of as not pulling our weight, spiritually speaking. The very concept of singleness is a threat to this ongoing aspect of the creation mandate. While some people can't help being single, maybe we should do all we can to keep that number of us as small as possible, and certainly not commend singleness.

But while it's undoubtedly true that I'm not directly helping to fill the earth, it's not the whole story. There are less direct ways in which we singles contribute to the fulfillment of the creation mandate. Multiplying and filling is more than simply reproducing. Many people who are unable to have children adopt. Many who never have children (either biologically or through adoption) nevertheless play a vital part in the care and nurture of others. I may not be directly causing population expansion, but I am a vital part of the growth of other people through friendship and involvement in their lives (just as they are a vital part of my growth). As we invest constructively in the lives of others, we are contributing tangibly to the creation mandate. Children need not only to be born but to be raised, taught, provided for, and nurtured. In most cases this needs more than just the parents. We may not be adding to the number of people out there, but hopefully we are contributing significantly to the quality of the people the earth is being filled with.

And it's not just children, of course. We continue to care for and nurture one another throughout our whole lives. This too is part of the "filling" process.

But there is another element in all this. The creation mandate needs to be read in the light of the Great Commission. The task given us at creation is now, because of the fall, somewhat incomplete. Humanity is in rebellion against its Creator, and the world has been cursed because of it. Genesis calls humanity to make more people, but Jesus calls his new humanity to make disciples (Matt. 28:19–20). For the earth to be filled with the image of God, people need to come into relationship with—and growing likeness of—the One who is the perfect image of God, Jesus Christ. We cannot fulfill the original intention of the creation mandate without reaching people with the gospel and building them up in Christ. This is where the mandate of Genesis 1 reaches its final fulfillment, and as we've seen, singles have a vital and distinct part to play in this as they give themselves to the family life of God's people and, through the work of the gospel, find themselves spiritually reproducing those who, like Paul with Titus, they can describe as a true son or daughter in the faith.

5

Singleness Hinders Ministry

Yesterday someone taught me how to play the game croquet. If you're not familiar with it, croquet involves using wooden mallets to hit wooden balls through hoops. It all looks quintessentially English. There's a nice lawn and people idling around, and occasionally someone clonks a ball here or there. You half expect to hear people talking about the colonies while one of the staff from *Downton Abbey* turns up with afternoon tea.

But beneath the genteel veneer it is all viciously tactical. Yesterday we played as two teams against each other. I'd just been whacking my ball as hard as I could in the direction of the next hoop, but apparently there's more to it than that. Waaay more. At one point my teammate stopped and admonished me: "If you want to go *fast*, go alone. If you want to go *far*, go together." I'd evidently been neglecting The Team.

He claimed it's a Chinese proverb, but according to recent research (me Googling it this afternoon), Al Gore said it was from Africa. But then in an episode of *30Rock* he also said he made that up. Either way it's the sort of thing that's the stuff of corporate teamwork seminars, in between chanting "There's no 'I' in team" and someone who sounds like Michael Scott from *The Office* telling you that TEAM stands for "Together Everyone Achieves More."

But it's also the kind of sentiment that lies behind a lot of thinking about single people and church ministry.

Do Pastors Have to Be Married?

The fact is, there aren't a whole lot of single people in pastoral ministry, and this sort of gets at why. *If you want to go fast, go alone. If you want to go far, go together.* This is, on many levels, entirely understandable. Scripture gives us the expectation that pastors will be married. Paul describes the requirements of those who would serve as pastors as follows:

> An overseer must be above reproach, the husband of one wife, sober-minded, self-controlled, respectable, hospitable, able to teach, not a drunkard, not violent but gentle, not quarrelsome, not a lover of money. He must manage his own household well, with all dignity keeping his children submissive, for if someone does not know how to manage his own household, how will he care for God's church? (1 Tim. 3:2–5)

Pastors need to have appropriate gifting (being able to teach) and appropriate character so as not to bring the gospel into disrepute. But alongside those two stipulations Paul adds that the pastor "must be the husband of one wife."

The passage itself provides some rationale for this. The church, like the family home, is a household. The pastor's track record in managing his own household will give some idea of how he will manage the life of the local church. The two are sufficiently analogous that ineptitude in the former damages credibility for being able to effectively cope with the latter. The stresses and strains of handling the dynamics and discipline of family life are a good testing ground for the larger-scale household management of pastoral ministry.

A similar rationale comes in Paul's letter to Titus:

> The husband of one wife, and his children are believers and not open to the charge of debauchery or insubordination. For an overseer, as God's steward, must be above reproach. He must not be arrogant or quick-tempered or a drunkard or violent or greedy for gain, but hospitable, a lover of good, self-controlled, upright, holy, and disciplined. He must hold firm to the trustworthy word as taught, so that he may be able to give instruction in sound doctrine and also to rebuke those who contradict it. (Titus 1:6–9)

Again, Paul's expectation is that pastors will be married. The pastor must be the husband of one wife, and someone whose own home life supports the credibility of his ministry. But there are reasons beyond this for why it might be to everyone's advantage that a pastor be faithfully married.

A friend of mine took up a role leading a Christian ministry, and it was clear from the beginning that there were going to be some significant challenges in managing the staff team and casting the right sort of vision for the ministry as a whole. I remember talking to him several months into the role, when he said how much his marriage had helped him cope with some of those challenges. He had, he said, so much more emotional capacity as a result of his marriage. He could cope with more than if he'd been on his own. His wife's emotional support and protection enabled him to work with challenges he likely would not have survived as a single man. If you want to go fast, go alone. If you want to go far, go together. Many others can testify similarly.

Christian leader Al Mohler reflected on the difference being married made to his early life as a pastor:

> I was called as pastor of a small country church when I was engaged to be married. This sweet church took a risk with a young seminary student who was anxious to be married and just waiting for the date to arrive. I can testify that my ministry was transformed the moment I showed up back at the church with Mary, my wife. My relations with church members of both sexes took on a much more natural shape, and this was amplified with married couples of all ages. When children came, my ministry in later years was also deepened and widened.[1]

Being married and having children makes it easier to identify with and minister to those with families in a local congregation. Little wonder that many churches look for new pastors to be people with families. In my own church the vast majority of members are married with children. It is a huge swathe of the church family to risk being unable to relate well pastorally.

It needs to be said that there are also less godly reasons some churches don't want to have single pastors. Some worry that there must be something wrong with or weird about a pastor who is not married. And, frankly, too many churches assume having a married pastor effectively means they're getting a second staff member for free.

Most churches do not put on their advertisements for pastors, "Single people need not apply," but it is easy to see why it might be harder for single pastors to find employment. One said this of his search for a pastorate: "Once I say I'm single, never married, I never hear back."[2] Many others would be able to say the same thing.

But we mustn't be too quick to rule out singles as pastors, even of a flock that is mostly married. In the passages quoted above, 1 Timothy 3:2–5 and Titus 1:6–9, Paul is commending marital fidelity rather than ruling out those who are not married. His expectation is that people will be married—and therefore need to be the right sort of married—rather than prescribing that they *must* be.

If we take those Scriptures as being wholly prescriptive, then we need to recognize that they are being prescriptive of far more than marriage. Both passages, after all, speak of the need for pastors to manage their children well. So if we're to be consistent, we need to rule out not only pastors who are not married but also pastors who are married but without children. And, strictly speaking, given that Paul talks about children as plural in both passages, we must also rule out pastors who have only one child. So if we think there is biblical warrant here for disqualifying pastors for being single, then we also need to disqualify pastors who are married but have fewer than two children, and (presumably) pastors who are widowed and no longer have a wife to be married to.

Can Single Pastors Serve Married People?

It is also not necessarily the case that singleness precludes being able to help those who are nonsingle. As I've said, the church I belong to is mostly married with children. When I first arrived there to be one of the pastors, I was conscious of this and wondered if it would be a significant hindrance to people being able to receive my ministry. What I discovered was that there were ways in which being single actually *helped*.

One of the things I've noticed as an Englishman who spends of lot of time doing ministry in the United States is that I am perceived as neutral on many of the intramural debates that happen within that part of the Christian world. I am not seen as particularly belonging to any one network or denominational tribe and can therefore move freely between them in a way that might not otherwise be easy. The distance I come from creates an openness to what I may be able to give. It's not that I don't have positions of my own on many of the matters these groups differ over, but coming into the discussion from "outside" provides an air of neutrality.

I've noticed a similar dynamic when it comes to ministering to people with families. I remember catching up with a couple from church who had recently had their first child. I asked them how it was all going, and from having spent lots of time with new parents I knew that being able to get sufficient sleep can be a significant challenge. So I was surprised by what they said about sleep: "Well, we can talk to *you* about this, but not to any of the other parents round here."

The fact is, they were getting plenty of sleep. Somehow (and they didn't have an explanation for this), their baby was sleeping the whole way through virtually every night. But they said it was the sort of thing that actually made things tense with other parents at church.

This was my introduction to the idea that there are certain ways being single makes it easier for people to talk about their experiences of marriage and parenthood. Sometimes they wish to talk about issues that are contentious among parents. I quickly learned that within the parenting world, there are any number of intramural disagreements: what kind of routine to establish for a baby; whether to follow this or that philosophy of early-childhood parenting; when, if, and how a mother should return to work; what sort of schooling is favored for a child. Disagreements over home schooling or state schooling or fee-paying private schooling quickly get very tense. And like lots of debates around parenting, people can take things personally. If people disagree with you, it feels like they're saying you're a bad parent, which, in a culture that prizes family self-sufficiency and therefore calls for virtual omnicompetence, is an accusation no one wants to receive.

It is not that I don't have opinions about any of these things, but as a single person I don't *appear* to, and certainly not to the point of investing my own flesh-and-blood progeny in any particular side. Sometimes not being a parent is better than being the type of parent other parents disagree with.

At other times some have the need to talk about struggles and failures in family life. Because of the belief that marriage means "happily ever after" or the prevailing views of our self-sufficient culture, it is easy for people to feel self-conscious about problems they might have in family life. "Surely marriage is meant to be the solution to my problems," they think, "so if I am really struggling maybe I'm not doing it right?" One couple admitted to me that they felt safer talking to me about their marriage because they feared that other married people would compare them to their own marriage and judge them.

Singleness can also make it easier to speak from the pulpit about some aspects of family life. One of my married pastor colleagues noticed that if he speaks on the hardships of marriage, church members start to wonder if it means he's having a difficult time with his own marriage at home. While it is good to be able to have experience to speak from, sometimes people assume it means you *must* be speaking from experience even if you're just making a general observation from Scripture.

This leads to something that is commonly overlooked. What matters most in ministering to marrieds and parents is not personal experience but faithfulness to Scripture. At the end of the day, what the congregation most needs to hear is not the wisdom a pastor might have accumulated over the years as a husband or father but *God's* wisdom revealed in his Word. It's worth saying that single people can often be guilty of the same mistake—feeling cynical any time a married pastor deigns to speak on singleness (even though any married pastor will have experienced singleness at some point).

If someone thinks it's laughable that I find myself preaching on passages directed to husbands and wives or to parents, they're assuming that human experience matters more than divine wisdom. It doesn't occur to many of them that the very passages they'd prefer to hear a married person speak from were in most cases written by an apostle who was himself single. I suspect that many churches that gladly have Paul as an apostle would not have appointed him as a pastor.

In churches with more than one teaching pastor, having at least one who is single can also be advantageous. If the primary examples of the Christian life that many of us see in church are always married ones, it can reinforce the idea that being married necessarily accompanies Christian maturity. It is good for church members to see examples before them of gospel-focused singleness as well as gospel-focused marriage. It is a way of demonstrating what Paul said about both marriage and singleness being honorable gifts of God.

Is Singleness Actually an Advantage in Ministry?

So pastors being single is not prohibited by Scripture, nor is singleness necessarily a hindrance to effective gospel ministry, even in contexts where the majority of people are married. But there is another reason that singleness might, in fact, be an advantage in ministry. Paul describes it at length in his famous treatment on marriage and singleness in 1 Corinthians:

> I want you to be free from anxieties. The unmarried man is anxious about the things of the Lord, how to please the Lord. But the married man is anxious about worldly things, how to please his wife, and his interests are divided. And the unmarried or betrothed woman is anxious about the things of the Lord, how to be holy in body and spirit. But the married woman is anxious about worldly things, how to please her husband. I say this for your own benefit, not to lay any restraint upon you, but to promote good order and to secure your undivided devotion to the Lord. (1 Cor. 7:32–35)

There was an obvious parallel for Paul and his readers here with the way many eunuchs served in the ancient world. For kings, eunuchs were desirable servants because they had no heirs. They would not be able to establish any rival dynasty to the king's. But more than that, as Barry Danylak writes:

> The eunuch was also a model of devoted service because he was without the distractions of marriage and family. No personal family matters competed for his allegiances. He could afford complete, unhindered loyalty to his king and his king's concerns.[3]

Danylak therefore wonders if Jesus commended the eunuchs (see Matt. 19:12) because "the historical figure of the eunuch was a *paradigmatic* model of what such undivided loyalty to the king looked like in the ancient world."[4]

Paul can therefore talk about the unmarried person being "anxious about the things of the Lord." What these "things of the Lord" are, Paul also describes as "how to please the Lord." There is a way a single person is able to give him- or herself to the work of God's kingdom that is unencumbered from the proper concerns that should occupy someone who is married. What this looks like clearly varies from person to person. Much depends on the skills and opportunities God has given us.

Personally speaking, I can see some clear ways in which singleness has enabled me to serve Christ that would not be the case if I were married. I am able to be away from home more easily; I don't have to think about the impact of my absence on a wife or children. This has meant that I've been able to serve in a much wider range of contexts and for greater periods of time than someone who is married. When I am at home, I can be more available to my church. It is easier to drop things at a moment's notice if there is an urgent need or someone who needs visiting. I am able to be freer with some of my weekends and evenings.

From a logistical point of view, it is much easier to be flexible as a single person than as a married one. Trying to get a young family out the door is virtually an all-day event. By the time things have been packed for every conceivable eventuality and the last kid has finally got her shoes and coat on, someone decides he now needs the bathroom, and by the time he's finished, someone else will too. I've seen parent friends of mine physically age in the time it takes to get a clutch of infants from one side of the front door to the other. Trying to maneuver a family is like trying to turn a Mack truck around.

By contrast, some of us singles can turn on a dime. The day of a friend's wedding a while ago, I suddenly realized I'd lost track of time and had only ten minutes to get ready and leave the house. The only challenge was working out what to do with the remaining four minutes once I was ready. Sometimes we singles can be not only more flexible but also more responsive than our married friends.

There is a danger here, of course. This kind of freedom, when it comes with enthusiasm for ministry and lots of energy, means we can neglect giving time we need to building up friendships and investing in community. I know many single people in Christian ministry who have struggled with this. Church events typically take place on weekday evenings and over the weekends, so this can restrict opportunities to develop and build ordinary friendships in the wider community. If singles live at home alone, then there is not the same built-in social unit that those with their own families can automatically fall back on. A quick meal with someone before heading out for an evening meeting, or even some snatched time with someone for a quick catchup, needs to be planned and arranged in advance. If we don't plan things ahead of time, a day off can easily roll around, and we find we have nothing to do, and it is too late to find someone to make plans with.

This can be even more difficult for those on the more introverted side of things. If we have invested heavily in others during the week, we may feel relationally "spent" by the time it comes to a day off, and it can be too easy to use the day to recover energy on our own. If this becomes habitual, then the lack of deep friendship and community will brew into a crisis. This is something churches need to give thought to, so that singles in pastoral ministry have enough time *and* sufficient relational capital set aside in a given week to build friendships.

Similarly, if the single person lives alone, sometimes the only time to realistically catch up on chores is a day off. Laundry, housework, grocery shopping, and fixing things around the house all take time, as many a housekeeper knows. Many in pastoral ministry have a spouse to help, a wife who doesn't work and who kindly carries most of this noble, God-honoring task.

Single pastors may need more than the standard time off from ministry in order to do this work. Some churches provide singles on their staff an extra half-day off from church work for this very reason. The danger otherwise is that churches might seek to maximize the flexibility of their singles without supporting them in these other areas. Provision by a church family for the singles on staff needs to go beyond mere remuneration.

In sum, singleness doesn't necessarily make someone better suited to church ministry. It is not better than being married, just as being married is not better than being single. God is so much smarter than we are. Someone like, say, Tim Keller would never have been so profoundly used by God were it not for his marriage to Kathy, who supports, sharpens, and grounds him. Nor would someone like, say, John Stott have been so profoundly used by God were it not for his singleness, enabling him to give himself so deeply to so many people in so many places. Just as marriage by itself isn't a qualification for gospel ministry, so also singleness by itself isn't a hindrance.

6

Singleness Wastes Your Sexuality

A friend of mine has an interesting spoon. (Bear with me.) It's slightly larger than a teaspoon and has a large hole in the middle, making it incapable of holding—let alone carrying—the sort of substance that typically requires a spoon. My friend has no idea where it came from. And so for entertainment he keeps it in his sugar bowl, waiting for unsuspecting guests to attempt productive engagement with it. Some will quietly (but unsuccessfully) persevere with it, not wanting to make a fuss and assuming the fault must somehow be theirs. Others will immediately point out how the spoon is ridiculous and insist on something better suited to the task at hand.

But the spoon, my friend eventually discovered, was an olive spoon. It was *meant* to be like that. The hole in the middle is to drain the fluid as you lift the olive to your mouth. You can't make sense of the way the spoon *is* without understanding what it's *for*. It is true of my friend's olive spoon and it is true of our sexuality.

This much is self-evident to just about everybody: we're sexual beings, and our sexuality is meant to mean something. I've not met anyone who disputes these two basic statements. But unless we know what our sexuality is for, we won't understand how it is meant to be used. The best we'll end up doing, like my friend with his spoon, is to try to get some passing entertainment from it. As it happens, the actual shape of the Bible points us to the purpose of why we're sexual beings.

Why God Gave Us Sexuality

Genesis famously opens with an account of God creating our world. The scale is sweeping and cosmic. We see the beginning of literally everything. Matter is formed, shaped, ordered, and regulated. Life in all its staggering variety is poured into the world. Yet even here, within such abundant and lavish variety, there is order. Things are made according to their kind (see Gen. 1:11–25). It is not just a mass of undifferentiated matter nor even a flat kind of uniformity. There are *kinds* of things and variety within those kinds. God is the master conductor, bringing in each section of the orchestra and adding it to the symphony of creation.

The climax of all this creative activity is the entrance of humanity. It is always easy to assume the climax of anything is the moment when we show up, but in this case such an assumption is clear from the text. Up until this point there has been a rhythm and pattern to the work of creation. We've had "let there be's," evenings and mornings, and "it was good's." This abruptly changes at the point when people come on the scene:

> Then God said, "Let us make man in our image, after our likeness. And let them have dominion over the fish of the sea and over the birds of the heavens and over the livestock and over all the earth and over every creeping thing that creeps on the earth."

> So God created man in his own image,
>> in the image of God he created him;
>> male and female he created them. (Gen. 1:26–27)

We notice the difference immediately. Rather than God simply announcing something into existence, there is a moment of divine deliberation. He verbalizes his intent to do something. And rather than the repeated "Let there be," we now have "Let us make." This is not routine. Something different is happening here, and it warrants special attention. God's involvement in this particular act of creation seems especially personal.

The reason why is immediately given. This creature, unlike anything else in creation, is going to be uniquely like God. If everything God makes is to some extent a reflection of who he is, it is the case with humanity in a way it is not with anything else. For the first time something is made that will image God in his own creation, something that will uniquely correspond to who he is and what he's like.

A significant aspect of this image bearing is highlighted for us in the passage: God makes us as male and female. One of the features of the creation account in Genesis 1 is the introduction of various pairings. N. T. Wright describes these as "binaries," and he writes, "It's all about God making complementary pairs, which are meant to work together."[1]

The account opens with heaven and earth, immediately alerting us to the fact that the physical world we see and touch is not where all the action happens. There is an above and beyond, and the pairing with the earthly indicates there is meant to be some kind of correspondence between these two spheres. As the account continues, we're introduced to further pairings: light and darkness, day and night, sea and dry land. All of these, we know from basic experience, interact with and complement one another. "And then the story reaches its great climax with the creation of human beings in the image of God: male and female together."[2] The relationship between this final pair, male and female, will provide a clue to what will happen with the first pair, heaven and earth. The account concludes with God resting on the seventh day, showing us that while we might be the climax of God's creative work, we are not the climax of creation itself; God's rest and satisfaction is.

What happens next would surprise us if most of us weren't so familiar with the text.[3] Having had the wide-angle view of creation, we find ourselves in a garden with a man and a woman. We go from the universal to the particular. Adam is created by God, commissioned by him, shown to be inadequate on his own, and is given Eve as his perfect counterpart. They are brought together, and the opening plotline of the Bible is a wedding:

> And the rib that the LORD God had taken from the man he made into a woman and brought her to the man. Then the man said,
>
> > "This at last is bone of my bones
> >   and flesh of my flesh;
> > she shall be called Woman,
> >   because she was taken out of Man."
>
> Therefore a man shall leave his father and his mother and hold fast to his wife, and they shall become one flesh. (Gen. 2:22–24)

The question is why. Given the grand scale of what has just happened, why are we now in what, by comparison, seems like a cramped garden, watching a man marry a woman? That this is where the Bible plotline starts is hugely significant. What happens between this man and this woman gives us insight into what God has planned for the universe. There is a pattern here. As Ray Ortlund puts it, "After the heavens and the earth come together in the first creation, a man and woman come together in the first marriage."[4] The union of the man and the woman in marriage is going to point us to the eventual union of heaven and earth in Christ. N. T. Wright sums it up neatly:

> The coming together of male plus female is itself a signpost pointing to that great complementarity of God's whole creation, of heaven and earth belonging together.[5]

This becomes more and more apparent as the Old Testament unfolds. God, we discover, is not just a moral authority bearing down on us or a sovereign ruling over us. He is a bridegroom wanting to win us.

The prophets frequently use marital language to describe God's relationship with his people; he is the groom, and they are the (frequently wayward) bride. When they turn from him in disobedience and worship other gods, they are committing spiritual adultery, something which provokes some of the most vivid and searing passages in the Bible.

When Jesus enters the stage in the Gospels, he refers to himself in the third person as "the bridegroom":

> People came and said to him, "Why do John's disciples and the disciples of the Pharisees fast, but your disciples do not fast?" And Jesus said to them, "Can the wedding guests fast while the bridegroom is with them? As long as they have the bridegroom with them, they cannot fast. The days will come when the bridegroom is taken away from them, and then they will fast in that day." (Mark 2:18–20)

In other words, Jesus is that same divine bridegroom who has been pursuing his bride all through the Old Testament. He has come not just to be a teacher, clarifying what had been misunderstood about God among the teachers of his people. He is not just an example of someone who knew how to live God's ways and embody God's purposes. He has come as a savior, and this shows us what *kind* of savior. He is not a savior who is happy only to lift us from the water, plop us back onto dry land, and be done with us, nor one merely willing to extend the act of saving into an ongoing kind of nodding acquaintance. As savior, he intends to be a *husband* to the people he's rescued.

This is reflected all through the New Testament. Paul reminds his readers that their relationship to Jesus is analogous to that of a sexual union between a man and a woman:

> Do you not know that he who is joined to a prostitute becomes one body with her? For, as it is written, "The two will become one flesh." But he who is joined to the Lord becomes one spirit with him. (1 Cor 6:16–17)

The "one flesh" union reflects something of the "one spirit" union believers have with Christ. In Ephesians Paul talks about marriage and how husbands and wives are to honor one another, and then he abruptly pulls back to show them that what he's really talking about is Jesus and the church:

> "Therefore a man shall leave his father and mother and hold fast to his wife, and the two shall become one flesh." This mystery is profound, and I am saying that it refers to Christ and the church. (Eph. 5:31–32)

The mystery behind human marriage is—as we now see it's always been—Christ's relationship to the church.

And, of course, at the very climax of Scripture we have the marriage supper of the Lamb and his people, followed by a vision of heaven and earth finally united as the new Jerusalem comes down from heaven to earth like "a bride adorned for her husband" (Rev. 21:2). Heaven and earth at last become united, and marriage is the language that best describes it.

Human marriage, then, reflects the big story of the Bible. As Ray Ortlund puts it, marriage "is the wraparound concept for the entire Bible."[6] It illustrates the big thing God is doing in the universe: making a people for his Son. Ortlund continues:

> The eternal love story is why God created the universe and why God gave us marriage in Eden and why couples fall in love and get married in the world today. Every time a bride and groom stand there and take their vows, they are reenacting the biblical love story, whether they realize it or not.[7]

And this story provides the key to understanding our sexuality.

This reminds us again of why the Bible repeatedly insists on the heterosexual character of marriage. For marriage to be a reflection of Christ and the church, it must be between like and unlike, male and female. Change this arrangement, and you end up distorting the spiritual reality to which it points. Alter marriage, and you end up distorting the gospel it is meant to portray.

N. T. Wright concludes an article on the heterosexual nature of marriage in this way:

> The biblical picture of man and woman together in marriage is not something about which we can say, "Oh well, they had some funny ideas back then. We know better now." The biblical view of marriage is part of the larger whole of new creation, and it symbolizes and points to that divine plan.

111

. . . Marriage is a sign of all things in heaven and on earth coming together in Christ.[8]

Having a Gospel-Focused View of Marriage

This vision of marriage helps us keep it in healthy perspective. Grasping what it points to means two things.

First, we won't demean or trivialize it. It points to Christ and his people. We'll therefore take it seriously. In the old language of the Book of Common Prayer, it "therefore is not by any to be enterprised, nor taken in hand, unadvisedly, lightly, or wantonly, to satisfy men's carnal lusts and appetites, like brute beasts that have no understanding; but reverently, discreetly, advisedly, soberly, and in the fear of God."[9] It matters and, married or not, all of us need to uphold it: "Let marriage be held in honor among all, and let the marriage bed be undefiled" (Heb. 13:4).

Given the unique dignity of marriage to reflect the gospel in this way, it is no surprise that so much of the health of a society depends on the health of its marriages. But while we have unique reason as Christians to esteem marriage, the very thing that grants it such special significance also protects us, second, from making too much of it. It is not to be idolized. Marriage is not ultimate, but it points to the thing that is. Marriage itself is not meant to fulfill us but to point to that which does. The real marriage is the one we find in Christ. Our marriages on earth are just the visual aid of this.

The original *Zoolander* movie has this as its central premise: the more good-looking you are, the more stupid you are. The main character, Derek Zoolander, is a "ridiculously good-looking" male model and therefore significantly endowed when it comes to stupidity. At one point in the movie, a group of people decide to build a school in his honor. They present him with their architectural model of what will eventually be constructed. Zoolander walks in, looks at the model, and is livid.

"Is this a school for ants?" he bellows at them. "It needs to be at least *three times* bigger than this!"

He thinks he is seeing the actual school. He has mistaken the model for the reality.

And we do the same with marriage very, very easily. We mistake it for the fuller reality and ultimate satisfaction to which it points. Even in our Christian circles, we do this All. The. Time. We expect from our earthly marriage what we will find only in our spiritual one.

One of the perks of being an ordained pastor is that I get to participate in weddings from time to time. It's a great privilege and usually a great encouragement. But over recent years I've noticed a growing and concerning trend: hearing someone (normally the groom) say things of his spouse that a believer should say only of Christ. Just recently I heard a Christian guy talking about his bride-to-be. By all accounts she is a wonderful Christian lady. But at one point he said, "She is the light of my world," and I suddenly felt very uncomfortable. The fact is, you are not loving your bride if you expect her to be something only Jesus can be. You may think you are honoring her, but in fact you are doing something profoundly unloving. She was not created to be the light of this man's world. She couldn't be even if she wanted to. He is putting a burden on her that she was never designed to bear. Putting it bluntly, if you marry someone expecting him or her to fulfill you, you're going to be a bit of a nightmare to be married to. You're demanding something only Jesus can deliver. You are thinking your marriage is what will fill your life and complete it. That will only disappoint you and utterly crush the poor soul you're married to.

A good friend of mine who has been happily married for over forty years recently said to me, "My marriage is much better than I ever expected or deserve it to be. But it is not enough." That wasn't a complaint. It was a healthy recognition of something that too many people (married or otherwise) are unaware of.

Several months ago I had the privilege of leading the wedding ceremony of a lovely young couple. It was an idyllic occasion, but in the middle of the sermon I felt led to say this to them: "If at some point you find your marriage is a disappointment to you, please bear in mind that's because it's supposed to be. It's not meant to fulfill you, but to point to the thing that does." Seeing this ultimate significance of marriage as pointing to our union with Christ is vital. Nothing gives marriage more dignity, but nothing better protects us from investing ultimate significance in it.

Having a Gospel-Focused View of Singleness

My first ride in an ambulance, like most people's, was completely unexpected. For a few days I'd been struggling with painful abdominal cramps, and assumed it was some form of food poisoning that would eventually subside. It wasn't and it didn't. The pains became more intense, so I went for a walk-in examination at my local doctor's. The waiting room was full; this wasn't going to be a quick visit. I sat there, doubled over in pain, and as soon as the doctor appeared to call in the next patient the entire room pointed to me and said, "You need to see him next." It takes a lot for English people to let someone skip the line.

About two minutes and one careful prod in the stomach was all it took for the doctor to realize what was wrong: my appendix was on the point of bursting. He sent for an ambulance and off I went. It was the most physical pain I'd ever been in, but it still felt kinda exciting to be in an ambulance, knowing it was speeding through traffic with the lights and siren blaring. Needless to say, once I was where I needed to be (on a surgeon's table) it was all very straightforward from there. A short convalescence back home and soon I was on my feet.

Life without an appendix, of course, is not something one has to adjust to. Other than now being a few ounces lighter, nothing changed. Whatever role it might once have played, it is now pretty much vestigial. The body works just fine without it. I haven't missed it at all.

It might be easy to think of our sexuality in similar terms. Given what we've seen about how marriage points to the relationship Jesus has with his people, where does that leave those of us who are unmarried? If we are to live lives of celibacy, does that mean our sexuality is now playing no active role in our lives? Are people like me wasting our sexuality by not giving expression to our sexual desires? If so, it seems odd that this vital aspect of our humanity is now seemingly redundant. If God made us sexual beings, how can it be good that we don't in any way fulfill that aspect of who we are? Our married friends can feel satisfied that they're honoring their sexual feelings, giving expression to them in a godly way and in the proper context of marriage, and thereby honoring their sexuality as it points beyond itself to its ultimate referent in Christ.

It is understandable to think this way. I have done so myself at various points, and regularly meet people who still do, especially singles. They feel as though this negation of sexual activity in some way makes them incomplete and dissatisfied. It doesn't feel right to have something so apparently significant just sitting there unutilized. It would be like a phenomenal pianist never having access to a keyboard. Seems like a waste. But this is not the full way the Bible would have us think about our sexuality. The meaning of marriage in no way exhausts the way in which our sexual desires, met or unmet, can play a constructive role in our lives and be a means of honoring the gospel.

On one occasion Jesus was asked about the nature of marriage in the coming kingdom of God. The Sadducees, who didn't believe in the resurrection of the dead, thought they had found a knockout blow to those who did:

> Teacher, Moses said, "If a man dies having no children, his brother must marry the widow and raise up offspring for his brother." Now there were seven brothers among us. The first married and died, and having no offspring left his wife to his brother. So too the second and third, down to the seventh. After them all, the woman died. In the resurrection, therefore, of the seven, whose wife will she be? (Matt. 22:24–28)

The Sadducees were referring to the Old Testament practice of levirate marriage. In the Old Testament, to die without children was a disaster. Children were not just one's legacy; they represented a spiritual inheritance and an ongoing place in the land God had promised. To the Sadducees, this practice made nonsense out of the belief that there was going to be a resurrection of the dead. We'll get to that in a moment, but we need to deal first with the fact that for many people today, this practice made a mockery of something closer to home: it implied that a childless widow was to be passed around the family line like an heirloom.

One of the things we need to realize is that in the Old Testament, this reflects not a low view of the first brother's wife but a high view of her—she was not to be left destitute. God had shown himself to be a redeemer of his people, and embedded in his law are commands that show that he wanted them to be redeemers too. For a man to marry his brother's widow meant she would have a place and inheritance among God's people. One of the most famous examples in Scripture is when Boaz married Ruth. He was her kinsman-redeemer, a member of her family who could legitimately redeem her. Taking on the responsibilities of kinsman-redeemer wasn't easy; it was a huge act of kindness and potentially very costly. (A relative closer than Boaz passed on redeeming Ruth for this very reason.) By doing so, Boaz points forward to the ultimate redemption that comes through Christ, the one who became our kin so that he could redeem us at great cost.

Back to the Sadducees. They have Jesus in what they think is a theological headlock. God's law itself made the idea of the resurrection untenable, as they think their hypothetical situation shows. But Jesus won't have it.

> Jesus answered them, "You are wrong, because you know neither the Scriptures nor the power of God." (Matt. 22:29)

They thought the Scriptures backed them up, but Jesus accuses them of biblical illiteracy. They don't actually know the Bible beyond the handful of verses they assume confirms their thinking. And more than that—they don't know the power of God. They've thought up a scenario that they are convinced a resurrecting God can't handle, a thought experiment God wouldn't have thought of. They have no sense that God's hand is so much bigger than man's. Their Scriptures are full of blank pages, and their God is no more powerful than what their imaginations can conceive of.

Jesus continues:

> For in the resurrection they neither marry nor are given in marriage, but are like angels in heaven. And as for the resurrection of the dead, have you not read what was said to you by God: "I am the God of Abraham, and the God of Isaac, and the God of Jacob"? He is not God of the dead, but of the living. And when the crowd heard it, they were astonished at his teaching. (Matt 22:30–33)

They didn't have microphones to drop in those days, but you get the idea. God's famous refrain throughout the Old Testament had clearly been lost on them. Just because Abraham, Isaac, and Jacob had died didn't mean that God was done with them. Their stories were not finished yet. He was still their God, and they were still his people. Only a small mind can imagine that God's promises and purposes are constrained by human life spans.

But the key point for us is the first one Jesus makes. There will be a resurrection—there will be a physical life to enjoy in the coming kingdom of God. And one of the characteristics is that there will no longer be human marriage. Jesus compares the way we will be then to angels. We mustn't miss the point he's making. We'll be like the angels, not in the sense of being all winged and floaty (he's talking about a physical resurrection, after all), but like them in respect to their marital status. The Sadducees had been mistaken in assuming (1) there would be no resurrection, and (2) that if there was a resurrection life, it would correspond exactly to life now. But the resurrection is not just an extension of our physical life; it is a transformation and fulfillment of it. And, says Jesus, that means (among other things) there will be no more marrying. That aspect of life, it turns out, belongs only to this realm.

We need to let this sink in. Jesus is not just saying that there won't be any more interminable photo shoots, or any more awkward wedding lines, or any more hokey father-of-the-bride speeches. He is saying that there will be no more earthly marriage. Marriage, as we practice it now, will have served its purpose. Life then is a fulfillment of all that marriage now is meant to point to.

My parents, like virtually all parents, have pictures of me and my brother in various prominent places around their home. I discovered recently that they always take along a couple of these pictures when they travel. Wherever they are, home or away, they like reminders of their family. But they don't bring them along when they take a trip with me or come to visit. When you have the physical reality, you don't need the picture.

Marriage is a picture of Christ and the church. So when we enter into the fullness of our relationship with him, when the church is finally presented to him as his perfected bride, the institution of marriage will have served its purpose. We will have the reality; we will no longer need the picture. As Glynn Harrison reminds us:

> The Bible does not teach that there will be no marriage in heaven. Rather, it teaches there will be one marriage in heaven—between Christ and his bride, the church.[10]

Our marriages are therefore temporal and momentary. They are not eternal. The state in which we will spend countless billions of years in ultimate bliss will not be as people married to one another. Outside of our relationship with Christ, we will be single. We can presume other forms of human connection will be present in the new creation. I take it that the friendships that lie at the heart of healthy marriages now will continue into eternity. But the marital constitution of them will not.

This reminds us that marriage now is not ultimate. It will be absent in the age to come and is not vital in this present time. This reality is reflected in the life of Jesus himself. The most fully human and complete person ever to live on this earth did so as someone who was single, and yet he called himself "the bridegroom." The marriage he came for was the one all of us who are in him will enjoy will him for eternity. His singleness on earth bore witness to this ultimate marriage he had come to establish.

Singleness for us now is also a way of bearing witness to this reality. Like Jesus, we can live in a way that anticipates what is to come. Singleness now is a way of saying that this future reality is so certain and so good that we can embrace it now. It is a way of declaring to a world obsessed with sexual and romantic intimacy that these things are not ultimate and that in Christ we possess what is.

> Single Christians who abstain from sex *outside* the marriage bond bear witness to the faithful nature of God's love with the same authority as those who have sex *inside* the marriage bond. . . . Denying yourself can be just as potent a picture of a thing's goodness as helping yourself to it. . . . Both single and married people who abstain from sex outside the marriage bond point to the same thing. They both "deploy" their sexuality in ways that serve as a sign of the kingdom and the faithful character of God's passion.[11]

If marriage shows us the shape of the gospel, singleness shows us its sufficiency.

This is why the church needs single people. Not as a supposedly endless source of free babysitting, but to remind us that the joy and fulfillment of marriage in this life is partial and can only be temporal. The presence of singles who find their fullest meaning and satisfaction in Christ is a visible, physical testimony to the fact that the end of all of our longing comes in Jesus.

But this doesn't mean our sexual feelings are redundant, dangling unfulfilled like the equivalent of an appendix. The sexual consummation we long for can (if we let it) point us to the greater consummation to come. Our sexual feelings remind us that what we forgo on a temporal plane now, we will enjoy in fullness in the new creation for eternity. Sexual unfulfillment itself becomes a means of deepening our sense of the fuller, deeper satisfaction we await in Jesus. It helps us to hunger more for him.

Glynn Harrison puts it this way:

> Whether we are married or single in this life, sexual desire is our inbuilt homing instinct for the Divine, a kind of navigation aid showing us the way home. You could think of it as a form of body language: our bodies talk to us about a greater reality of fulfillment and eternal blessing, and urge us to go there.[12]

This is liberating. It means my sexual feelings don't need to be met for their purpose to be fulfilled. When I feel that deep sense of longing, that feeling of sexual restlessness and frustration, I am to think of that ultimate restlessness that comes when we live apart from our Creator, a restlessness that has its answer in the one who promised deep and abiding rest for all who come to him. Sexual sin feels like the answer to that restlessness, but like all of sin's pleasures, it is only temporary and fleeting.

Celibacy isn't a waste of our sexuality; it's a wonderful way of fulfilling it. It's allowing our sexual feelings to point us to the reality of the gospel. We will never ultimately make sense of what our sexuality is unless we know what it is for—to point us to God's love for us in Christ.

7

Singleness Is Easy

It wasn't the conversation any of us had expected.

I was in New York City, visiting a church I regularly attend when I'm in town. Two friends and I happened to be sitting near each other at church that morning and got chatting after the service ended. None of us had lunch plans, so we decided to grab some food together, and before long we were deep in conversation about our experiences of singleness. I need to point out that single people don't forever talk about their singleness. In my experience, most of us don't talk about it enough. Remarkable about this conversation was not that we were talking about it, but that we were doing so in such an open way.

I don't recall how the topic came up, still less how it got on to the fears each of us had around our own singleness, but once we'd started, it was hard to stop. I hadn't ever spoken about these things before, and I'm not sure my two friends had either. It was raw but also cathartic. By the end we felt exhausted but also relieved—relieved to have been able to have the conversation, and relieved that none of us was alone in experiencing the anxieties we gave voice to. C. S. Lewis once said that friendship typically begins when someone says, "What, you too? I thought I was the only one!"[1]

So far in this book, I've been trying to respond to the many ways in which I think singleness is undervalued. Throughout the history of the church, the pendulum has swung one way and then the other when it comes to whether marriage or singleness is most worthwhile or spiritual. Today there is little doubt which way it has swung: we have an enormous tendency to undervalue biblical singleness in the church and wider culture. So, much of the corrective involves showing how singleness isn't as awful as we tend to think it is.

The danger of this exercise is that we end up thinking singleness is just a blast. Reading earlier chapters might have left some of us thinking singleness is just a constant festival of deep and interesting friendships and freedoms—none of the constraints and heartaches of family life, no significant other with whom to discuss every plan and idea, fewer dependents to feed and clothe. Singleness can sound much more fun and much less expensive.

Marriage and singleness, as I hope we've seen, are both good gifts from God, ways in which we can experience God's goodness, but in a fallen world they're gifts that come with unique difficulties. Neither is easy. Both are painful. Each has its ups and downs, and the ups and downs of each look different to those of the other. So the danger is that we compare the downs of our own situation with the ups of the alternative. We singles easily look at the ups of marriage and compare them to the downs of singleness, and it is just as easy for married people to do the same in reverse.

So having spent time necessarily underlining the (often overlooked) ups of singleness, we need to look at some of the downs. These cover everything from minor inconveniences to the kind of anxieties my friends and I discussed that lunchtime, which can keep us up at night.

The Difficulties of Singleness

There are the everyday things. Christian leader and writer Kate Wharton says this:

> When we have to fill in a form and tick a box marked "single"; when we have to pay a single room supplement for a holiday; when we are faced with "2 for 1" supermarket offers that we know we'll end up throwing away; when we steel ourselves to enter a party alone; when we need someone to hold the other piece of flatpack furniture we're building; when we come home to an empty house and there is no one to tell about the highs and lows of our day—at these times, and at many others, being single can feel like the raw end of the deal.[2]

None of these particular examples feels like a big deal on its own. But life is often the sum of trivial things, and the small details eventually add up and can have a large cumulative effect. Sometimes it is the small everyday things rather than the big dramatic moments that can be most painful. It's the little daily reminders that we are doing on our own what feels like we should be doing with others. At times these are easy to brush aside, and we can just get on with things. But at other times it can feel overwhelming.

My good friend Ed Shaw describes times when the pain of singleness feels unbearable. He calls these times "kitchen floor moments":

> I call them that because they involve me sitting on my kitchen floor. But I'm not doing something useful like scrubbing it,

although it could always benefit from that. Instead I'm there crying. And the reason for my tears is the unhappiness my experience of same-sex attraction often brings. The acute pain I sometimes feel as a result of not having a partner, sex, children and the rest.[3]

Ed Shaw's experience is not unique to those who are single because of same-sex attraction, as he is. Many know the pain of going without "a partner, sex, children and the rest," whatever the reason for their singleness might be.

I remember when I turned twenty imagining what life would be like by the time I turned thirty. My ambitions seemed fairly modest at the time: I hoped I would be in some form of pastoral ministry and that by then, I would also be married and a father. I figured it was the kind of aspiration that pleases God and that he'd therefore enable it. I turned forty not too long ago. Needless to say, things don't turn out the way we always expect or hope.

We all know that, of course. But there can come particular times when we begin to realize we're not where we'd hoped and expected to be. That's a painful threshold to cross. There was a season in my twenties when it seemed everyone I knew was getting married. It seemed that every Saturday between May and September was yet another wedding with the same group of guests, my same crumpled suit, and me feeling more and more like an endangered species as the only single in a world increasingly full of couples. There was the speculation about who would be next. Then there came the well-meaning but slightly awkward speculation about when my turn might come. But even worse than people speculating about when you might get married is when they eventually give up speculating about when you might get married. And worse than the realization that life isn't going according to how you'd planned is when you begin to realize that it *probably never will.*

Aside from not meeting your own expectations is the issue of not meeting those of people around you. In the secular world, people are waiting longer and longer to marry. But in the Christian world, it is still a rite of passage, one of the signs you've grown up.

I remember a friend of mine getting married while we were both at seminary, after which the professors began treating him differently. If I ever asked for an extension to a deadline for a paper or to be excused from a class, there was a virtual inquisition. But my friend's being married meant he was given immediate permission, no questions asked. It was as if he'd joined an exclusive club and just needed to flash the "Married" card to be given a free pass on everything.

Another friend of mine had had a tricky relationship with his father for many years. His dad, being a high achiever, was constantly frustrated that his son was not rising up the ranks as rapidly and as far as his old man thought he should. But that changed overnight when my friend got engaged. He couldn't understand why his father was treating him so differently. But it was obvious. Getting engaged, in his dad's eyes, meant that he had finally grown up. It was as if he'd suddenly aged ten years. Marriage was a sign of maturity. So remaining unmarried can alter how others perceive our maturity, and we feel the pain of that perception.

Doubtless there are those for whom immaturity is the reason for prolonged singleness. Perpetual adolescence is an increasing issue in the West. But some using singleness as an excuse to avoid the responsibility of marriage does not mean that singleness is the problem or that all who remain single are necessarily so for that reason. I remember being at a wedding once when an older man turned to me and said, "Are you *still* single?"

Being single in our twenties and early thirties can be wildly different from being single in our late thirties and forties. In our twenties, life can easily seem like an episode of *Friends*. Most of our friends are not yet married, and it is relatively easy to be in and out of one another's lives on a daily basis. Students have a few years of sharing dorms or houses with good friends; everyone is around and available. You don't really have to do anything on your own if you don't want to. Friendship is on tap. Even the mundane things—laundry, running errands, housework, cooking—end up being done with others. There is a wonderful camaraderie to it.

But once peers get into serious relationships and then marry, the dynamics of friendship can change dramatically. The basic unit of the social life shifts from a group of friends to couples. The frequency with which you see one another changes too. Friends you formerly saw virtually every day, you start seeing only once a week, then maybe once a fortnight, then once a month, and eventually only occasionally. Marriage isn't the only reason; there's an adjustment from a flexible student life to a less flexible work life, maybe with a commute added in too. But few things change friendship quite as dramatically as marriage.

To an extent, this is entirely appropriate. Marriages require time to grow effectively. But the moment someone enters a serious relationship, all other friendships can be significantly demoted. I think of one guy who was a great friend of mine during my early twenties. We got together multiple times a week. And then he started dating, quickly got married, and just *disappeared*. I never saw him. He was like Frodo from *Lord of the Rings*—the moment he put a ring on, he vanished. I've seen this happen a few times. Once a serious relationship is established and a couple gets married, friendship with others becomes a low priority. With one friend, this was worsened because it was his wife who tended to arrange what little socializing they did, and typically it involved her friends rather than his. One thinks of the response to the invitation from a character in one of Jesus's parables: "I just got married, so I can't come" (Luke 14:20 NIV).

It is no surprise that weddings can be a little bittersweet for single people. We're genuinely happy for our friends as they marry, but there can also be a sense of loss. It is the start of a new era for the couple, but the end of an era for our friendship. A single friend of mine in his late forties recently said that the marriage of one of his closest friends "felt like a bereavement." It feels as though you've been demoted.

One writer, Carrie English, describes feelings of rejection that come when attending the wedding of friends:

> Two people announcing publicly that they love each other more than they love you. . . . There's no denying that weddings change friendships forever. Priorities have been declared in public. She'll be there for him in sickness and in health, till death do they part. She'll be there for you on your birthday or when he has to work late.
>
> Being platonically dumped wouldn't be so bad if people would acknowledge you have the right to be platonically heartbroken. But it's just not part of our vocabulary. However much our society might pay lip service to friendship, the fact remains that the only love it considers important—important enough to merit a huge public celebration—is romantic love.[4]

Even when a friendship is maintained with a married friend, it often becomes lopsided. The married friend no longer needs you as much as he or she did. My observation is that most friendships involving someone single and someone married are significantly asymmetrical. I have seen this in three main ways.

First, it tends to be me, as the single person, who takes most of the initiative in the friendship. This is not always the case; I can think of a couple of married friends who will want to poke me in the ribs the moment they read this. But with many of my friendships, I tend to make the first move. This is understandable, as I am the one looking for some company when I have a free evening or weekend. My married friends don't have the same need for immediate company. I get that. But over time it can start to hurt, and it can make you wonder how long you might have to wait for them to initiate contact. Some of my friends have said something along the lines of, "You know where we are, and you're always welcome. Don't wait for us to invite you." On one level, this is very touching. But when several say it, the cumulative effect, on darker days, is to make me hear it as, "We're not going to be thinking of you or pursuing you. We don't necessarily *need* you. And so you're going to have to reach out to us if you want to come over. And it will always need to be you coming to us rather than the other way around." This leads to the next point.

Second, it tends to be me, the single, visiting them, the married. And, again, this is mostly understandable. It is easier for one person to travel to two than for two to travel to one. This is even more so when you factor in children; it is exponentially harder for all of them to come to me. I've seen families trying to leave the house. D-Day looked more straightforward logistically. I get that. And, as a number of children have discovered, my toy collection tends not to compare to theirs. When I want to cook dinner for married friends with kids, I'll often offer to cook it at their home. I know some friends' kitchens better than my own. That's not a problem; I love doing that. It means we're actually likely to get much more time together than if they had to wait until after the kids were sorted for the night in the care of a babysitter.

Similarly, there are some close friends who live far away. I'm thinking of the couple who recently gave me a key to their apartment in New York City and another American family who moved to England but managed to move to the wrong end of it. In both cases, my work takes me to their neck of the woods quite often, so I wouldn't expect to see them on my doorstep nearly as often as they find me on theirs.

The issue is friends who *could* visit but never actually do. I have married friends living in close proximity—even some without kids—who rarely come to my home. The problem is what this communicates—that while they like having you occasionally guest star in their lives, they're not necessarily interested in being part of yours, in getting to know your home and life and church and friends. It can become lopsided. Seeing someone in their own setting is a way of getting to know them much more fully. You see where and how they do life and get to know the people they do life with. After entering into someone's world, you find yourself asking about their friends and family members. You know who their pastor is and can laugh about some of the idiosyncrasies of their church family. This is what enables someone to feel truly known. If no one enters into our world, we can feel like mere accessories in others' lives.

Both these points—the fact that singles most often initiate get-togethers and experience them in the world of their married friends—are often expressions of the third asymmetry, and also a deeper and often more painful one. The fact is, in all likelihood, singles need their married friends more than their married friends need them. That's not to say that married friends don't need their single friends at all; it's just a different kind—or a different level—of need. As a single person, my friends are a lifeline. They're like family. They are the ones with whom I feel most known and loved. Some are members of my church; others are long-term friends who live elsewhere and I know from different contexts. I need them. Hugely. But the fact is, they don't need me in the same way. Many of them are the equivalent of family, but since they have families of their own, the familial sense I have toward them is not necessarily reciprocated. That might be good and right, as far as it goes, but it can also be painful at times.

I recently visited a close friend, and as I was leaving, we talked about when we would next see each other.

"When are you free?" I asked.

"I guess we're probably looking at three months' time," he said. Life was busy.

I was heartbroken. *Three months' time?*

A bit of context: he is one of my closest friends, and he's said many times that I am one of his. We've known each other for many years. In fact, few people know each other as well as we do and enjoy such openness. It's a rare gift. His home is a seventy-five-minute drive from my home, and that's not merely down the street, admittedly. But it's not like we have to cross time zones to see each other. I've driven farther than that just for a good curry.

Three months seemed a very long time. Life was busy—I get that. But it wasn't that he was heading overseas or preparing to go through a major life event such as having a baby or moving to a new home. It was normal stuff making life so busy rather than anything exceptional. What hurt was that he seemed kind of fine with the three-month interim. He said it in a somewhat apologetic tone. Yet while it wasn't ideal to him, it clearly wasn't a huge problem either. It felt like he was saying he could quite easily do without me. No biggie. But I can't get by with seeing such close friends only once every three months. It made me realize that while my close friends feel essential to me, I might not necessarily feel essential to them. That can really hurt. What they are to me, their families are to them. I exist much lower down their list of needs.

That becomes all the more apparent if and when they end up moving away. I am close to a family that lives a five-minute walk from my house. We've been good friends for years. We eat together once a week on average. We've gone on holidays together. We've known each other well enough and long enough to have developed a natural ease and familiarity with one another. They're the kind of people I can quite happily spend time with doing nothing at all. I'm quite serious. It's not unusual to find us sitting together all reading books and barely talking for a couple of hours or so. We have an unspoken rule that it's entirely okay to doze off on each other's couches. (I remember one occasion we spent most of an afternoon all sitting in the living room dozing at the same time. It was glorious.) More than once I've taken myself around to their house just to sit at their kitchen table to do some work while they were getting on with whatever they were doing.

Some of this might just be my personality type, but having people to do nothing with is quite important for singles. There are times when I feel emotionally tired but really want company, so it's great to have friends you see often enough that you don't need to spend your time together just catching up. If one problem is friends you *barely* get to catch up with, another is friends you *only* catch up with. It's easy for married friends to forget this, because they already have people to do nothing with, and having people with whom to do nothing is not necessarily a need they're conscious of.

All this to say that I am terrifically close to the family around the corner. I'm writing this while on a ministry trip to Australia. Due to some truly bad planning on my part, I was alone on my birthday last week while in transit. Knowing I'd be spending my birthday alone, the daughter of this family made me a quiz to do on the plane. I opened it up and saw that there were ten rounds of ten questions. Some rounds were about stuff she knows I am interested in (*Star Wars*, US politics, Thai food), but most were about things we'd done together—trips we'd taken, and even a whole round just on funny things her dad had said and done (like when we lost him on vacation in Central Park because he accidentally joined a group of German cyclists, or when he nearly drove us all off a cliff in the Pyrenees). It made me realize just how much life we'd done together over the years.

I share so much about this friendship to give you a sense of the pain I feel at the prospect of their move away—not to the next town or even the next county, but to another part of the country several hours away. In fact, they're moving while I'm on this trip. I'm gutted. They'll still visit me, and I'll still visit them, but because of the distance we'll only be able to manage it when we have at least a couple of spare days to make the journey. Gone are the spontaneous get-togethers after church, or the times when I've needed someone on whom to try out a new recipe, or when they've needed a guest to justify lighting the fire. Gone are the times when they've invited me during a busy work season to come and eat and then run, even texting me as they were about to serve up so I could come around just in time. It's hard to imagine not having them nearby anymore. I know that for the next few months it's going to sting whenever I walk past their road.

When such friends move (and if you'll excuse the cliché), it feels like they're taking a bit of my home with them. And when this happens a number of times over successive years, I feel like I'm Voldemort with relational Horcruxes scattered all over the place.

A couple of summers ago I experienced the double-whammy of two close friends moving overseas, each for work-related reasons. As it happens, they were probably the two people from among all my friends who most took initiative in getting together. Their going hasn't meant they've dropped off the map. I still get to see them. Each of us has been able to visit the other, sometimes more than once. And because of the distance, when we do see each other now, it is typically for a few days rather than a few hours, so we are able to get well beyond just quickly catching up. But it's not the same as having them in easy reach. Each lived less than an hour away from me before they moved. One of them (who was single and therefore a bit more mobile) I would see pretty much weekly, often at short notice if one of us was at a loose end and in the mood for company. It's that week-to-week nature of proximate friendship that I've missed the most since they've moved. I'd give anything to have them back in the area.

But more than that, a friend moving away is hard because of what it often represents. People move for all sorts of reasons: a new job, proximity to family; cost of living. But whatever the reason, it is another way of reminding us that however close our friendship is, it's not close enough to make someone think twice about upping sticks and moving off. Even what had been in some cases the most porous family boundary is now suddenly hardened. The family goes. You stay. That's the deal. Now, I'm not complaining about that or denying that there is no distinctive obligation that comes with having a blood family. But the exercise of those very obligations is a reminder that what your friends have with their families, they don't have with you, and you might not have with anyone.

People will move for family or for economics, but no one moves for friends. All of this underlines the fact that there's a commitment that comes with family that is lacking in the way most people think about friendship.

There are times when these pains can be overwhelming. A couple of years ago I had a bit of a meltdown. It had been brewing for a while. I was serving in a church role that had become increasingly difficult for me to do, and I had ministry responsibilities in broader contexts that altogether were taking me beyond my emotional capacity. I was recovering from a nasty virus and wrestling with post-viral fatigue. I had very little energy or strength, and I was beginning to sink.

But the trigger for the real downward spiral was seemingly innocuous. I was preparing to change jobs in a few months' time. The plan was to stop working for my church and start full-time with a different Christian ministry. While I didn't need to leave the area (or even leave my church), I did need to find another place to live—not in another town or another community but someplace in my hometown. It was hardly going to be a life event.

But in my sleep-deprived and increasingly anxious mind, this move began to represent something unavoidable and sinister. I was (it vividly seemed) looking for a house in which I would live alone and eventually die. It sounds a little silly now, a couple of years later and in a happier frame of mind, but I can still reach back in time and feel my way into that mind-set. I was dreading old age. It was as though the future had telescoped into the present, and lonely old age was about to come upon me. I lay awake wondering who I'd do life with then, and who would look after me. I wondered if anyone would even notice if I fell down the stairs and couldn't get up. I could imagine (and at some points couldn't stop imagining) being one of those people who dies but no one notices for weeks until the mailbox overflows or the smell gets too bad.

What was driving these intense anxieties that were blown out of proportion was the feeling that even close friendships had become provisional. There are no guarantees, since people can move at any point, or marry, or have some other commitment that supersedes their friendship with me. So, I reasoned, no matter how fond of me a good friend seemed to be, they would drop me when work or family warranted it.

This anxiety reached full volume, and there was nothing I could do to turn it down. It was the lens through which I saw everything. Even the encouragement of others during this time seemed to reinforce the anxieties. When one friend said, "Sam, as long as I'm in Maidenhead, you have a friend you can turn to," all I heard was that he would be my friend only until he moved, which (in my head) he inevitably would. Another friend said, "You know where we are. Don't wait to be invited," and what that told me was they weren't going to think of me enough to initiate an invitation; I would have to approach them. Someone else told me I was welcome in their house anytime for the next couple of days but not after that as they had family coming to stay, which reminded me that I wasn't part of their *real* family. It became all-consuming, and I was unwell for some time.

Thankfully the intensity of those anxieties subsided. I was given some time off work. I sought help. I turned to the Psalms and learned something of what it means to know God as a refuge. Things got better. I started to appreciate again the friendships I had rather than focusing on what I thought I lacked.

But those anxieties, while thankfully diminished, have never really gone away. There are times when they still trouble me. When I sat having that impromptu lunch with two friends from church in New York, we started to share our particular fears about long-term singleness. It was cathartic to do so, and I was helped to find out I wasn't the only one to feel these concerns. We also started to share what helps us get through times of anxiety and to keep a healthy perspective. For me, there are certain things I repeatedly need to remind myself of.

The Trustworthiness of God

I am grateful to my friend Kathy Keller for reminding me that God doesn't give us hypothetical grace but only actual grace. The point is that when we imagine all those worst-case scenarios, we are imagining them without factoring in the presence and grace of God that would be there if they actually happened. As Kathy wrote in an email once, "God doesn't play that game. He doesn't inject hypothetical grace into your hypothetical nightmare situation so that you would know what it would actually feel like if you ever did end up in that situation."[5] He only gives grace for our actual situation. Replaying these scenarios over and over in our mind is therefore not at all helpful and actually factors *out* what God would be doing were it to ever happen. What we're imagining is actually life in that situation without God's presence. Better to find something else to fill our minds with. C. S. Lewis makes a similar point when he says, "Remember one is given the strength to bear what happens, but not the 101 different things that might happen."[6]

One of the Scriptures I found myself returning to during that time of meltdown, and which is still a wonderful comfort, is Psalm 139 and these well-known words:

> O LORD, you have searched me and known me!
> You know when I sit down and when I rise up;
>   you discern my thoughts from afar.
> You search out my path and my lying down
>   and are acquainted with all my ways.
> Even before a word is on my tongue,
>   behold, O LORD, you know it altogether.
> You hem me in, behind and before,
>   and lay your hand upon me.
> Such knowledge is too wonderful for me;
>   it is high; I cannot attain it. (Ps. 139:1–6)

In this psalm David is reveling in how thoroughly God knows him. It sounds almost claustrophobic.

Some read these words and find them sinister and threatening, as though we are constantly under a menacing divine surveillance. But in fact they are liberating. During the height of my anxiety I saw a counselor and was able to gain some insight into what was fueling it all. I began to understand my fears and how they were affecting me. It gave me enough of a foothold to be able to know something of how to respond to them. This was hugely helpful. But even now I can't pretend to have gotten my head fully around it all. All of us are deep waters; some of our fears go back a long way. We're complicated creatures. We can't always get to the bottom of our insecurities and pains.

So it is a great comfort to know that God has searched us and knows us. He is able to see into us far beyond our own capacity to do it. All that we can't understand about ourselves God is not only aware of but knows thoroughly and intimately. He knows my fears better than I do. And he knows my needs better than I do. When I am anxious, it is because I'm worried God doesn't know what I actually need and might not pull through for me. I worry that he might not provide the friendship and companionship I long for, or that he might not know how much I need this and might somehow overlook it. So this is what I cling to and tell myself repeatedly:

> God knows me more than I know myself.
> God loves me more than I love myself.
> God is more committed to my ultimate joy than I am.
> So I can trust him.

I also remember that the provisionality I both feel and fear about friendship applies to everything else as well. It is actually no less true for married people. Not all marriages survive. Spouses die. I know people who have lost spouses relatively early. Getting married is no guarantee of companionship and care for life. Neither is having kids. Life in this tragic and fallen world is fraught for all of us. No one situation provides any ultimate security. Whatever our station in life, we live with uncertainty. It's not a problem of singleness; it's a problem of life. The only guarantee is that Christ will never leave us or forsake us. He is the only one we can be sure will stick by us.

> Even though I walk through the valley of the shadow of
>   death,
>   I will fear no evil,
> for you are with me;
>   your rod and your staff,
>   they comfort me. (Ps. 23:4)

This is the part of Psalm 23 no one puts on inspirational posters. We're not in lush meadows and green pastures now. We're in the grittiness of life. We're reminded not just that Christ is with us through all of life, but that there are some places *only* Christ can accompany us. In the darkest recesses of the valley of the shadow of death Christ will be with us. Not even the closest friend or spouse on earth can walk with us through death. At some point on our journey, every human friend will leave us and be unable to accompany us any farther.

As I reflected on these passages and truths, it began to dawn on me that what I was actually craving in my soul is not found in the best of earthly friends or the greatest spouse. I realized that even if I had the best kind of friends this world could offer, it wouldn't be enough. It never could be. Our deepest aches and yearnings for intimacy will only ultimately be met in Christ. That's not to minimize the importance and goodness of friendship in this world, whether in marriage or outside of it. Such human intimacy is a wonderful gift from God and something each of us needs. But while we don't want to minimize this, we do need to relativize it. It will never be ultimate. We will always need something that is whole levels of magnitude more.

Think back to that friend of mine who said that his marriage "is much better than I ever expected or deserve it to be. But it's not enough." He wasn't indicating a deficiency in his marriage; he was recognizing the limits of even the best kind of intimacy this life has to offer. If marriage is actually the answer to our deepest longings and needs, then it turns out all the married people I know aren't doing it right. As Andrea Trevenna writes, "Ask an honest, married Christian, and they'll tell you that marriage cannot bear the weight of having all our hopes, dreams and longings placed upon it."[7]

When we realize this, we make an important discovery. The key to contentment as a single person is not trying to make singleness into something that will satisfy us; it is to find contentment in Christ as a single person. The key to contentment as a married person is not trying to build a marriage that can make us content; it is to find contentment in Christ as a married person. This is liberating. It means that my contentment is not contingent on my marital status, or on the number and depth of my friendships. These are not the most significant determiners of what will make life ultimately work. We need to consider the force of these words of Jesus:

> I am the bread of life; whoever comes to me shall not hunger, and whoever believes in me shall never thirst. (John 6:35)

I've read those words many times over the years, and largely missed the point of them. I always read it as though Jesus was just adding yet another line to his résumé. We've got that he's the Good Shepherd, and the way, the truth, and the life. Now we can add to the list that he's also the Bread of Life. But Jesus is not the Bread of Life simply in *addition* to all the other things he is, but in *opposition* to all the other things we're tempted to mistake for it. He's not informing me; he's rebuking me.

We miss this because we don't understand bread. The problem is that bread is something we like but not something we need. I had lunch out with a friend recently, and the waiter came and offered us some bread for the table. We declined, preferring to wait for the food that was coming. So when we hear Jesus say, "I am the bread of life," we think he's asking if we would like a bit of religion for the table.

In Jesus's time (and in some places today) bread was a staple. People ate it all the time, not because they were all crazy about bread but because, for the most part, bread was all there was to eat. No bread meant no life. You'd spend the hours of your day working to make sure you'd have bread to eat. If you didn't have bread, you died. It was as simple as that. So when Jesus says he's the bread of life, he's saying that he's to our soul what bread is to a starving stomach. He's saying he is the only one who can satisfy us at the very deepest level. It's a way of saying that all the other things we're tempted to think are crucial to getting life right are *not*. Sex. Marriage. Romance. Deep friendship. It's not that they don't matter at all, but that they don't matter that *much*.

One thing that has changed in my life because of this is something I barely even noticed. Early on as a Christian I prayed fervently for the gift of marriage. I was desperate for it. But some time ago I noticed that it had been a long time since I'd prayed for it. I hadn't consciously decided to pray for it less; it had just gradually become less and less important to me, and without realizing it, I wasn't thinking about it as much anymore. Marriage didn't become less good; it just became less significant. I was realizing that, as a Christian, there isn't anything ultimate I am missing out on by being unmarried. It is a good gift from God, but not an essential or necessary gift. What I most need I already have in abundance. I was starting to find my contentment in Christ.

None of this necessarily makes singleness easier. The difficulties are still difficult. At some point, another really good friend will tell me he's decided to move to Uzbekistan, or someone will get married and disappear off the grid. It might be that I end up having to move away and start from scratch somewhere else. All these things will hurt deeply. There may be times ahead when circumstances feel unbearable again. I'm not going to pretend future meltdowns won't happen. But I know that it's not my capacity and strength I need to depend upon. It's God's. Think of these wonderful words Paul prayed for his friends in Ephesus:

> That you may know . . . what is the immeasurable greatness of his power toward us who believe, according to the working of his great might that he worked in Christ when he raised him from the dead and seated him at his right hand in the heavenly places, far above all rule and authority and power and dominion, and above every name that is named, not only in this age but also in the one to come. (Eph. 1:18–22)

Paul is praying that his friends would know something of the greatness of God's power. It is immeasurable. We are able to measure the strength of all sorts of things. I can tell you about the world's most powerful drink, the most powerful chili sauce, the most powerful poison, the most powerful bomb ever detonated. All these things are stupendously strong. But they can all be measured. In each case there is a scale or measurement, a means of determining their strength compared to other things. But God's power is immeasurable. There is no unit of measurement and no scale that can be applied to it.

Paul says this strength has been fully demonstrated once before. God has flexed this muscle in the past, when he took Jesus from the grave and exalted him to the heights. This power could break death to pieces and thrust Christ to the ultimate supremacy. Listen to how Paul describes him: Jesus is "far above all rule and authority and power and dominion, and above every name that is named." You got that? There is literally no room for anyone else there. And in case we spotted some potential wiggle room, Paul adds, "not only in this age but also in the one to come." No one comes close to Jesus. No one ever will. This is ultimate and irreversible, unsurpassable and permanent. And God's power did it. *That* is how strong God is.

There's an old joke about the pope making an official visit to New York City. He arrives, and as he makes his way to the car, he insists that the driver get in the back and let the pope drive. This is against all protocols and procedures, but the driver has no choice but to obey. If the pope wants to drive, so be it. Well, in his enthusiasm to be behind the wheel, the pope ends up speeding, and a traffic officer pulls him over to book him, realizes it is the pope, and makes a panicked call to his captain.

"Boss, I've got a situation. I've just pulled someone over for speeding, but he's really powerful."

"Is it the mayor?"

"No. More important."

"The governor of the state?"

"Even greater."

"Wait, are you telling me you've pulled over the president of the United States?"

"He's even more important than that."

"Then who is it?"

"I've no idea. But the *pope* is his driver!"

If that's who's in the front of the car, it beggars belief who might be in the back. Well, if that is how supreme Jesus is, just imagine how powerful God must be to have exalted him in this way. And that is the power Paul is praying his readers will know about. This piece of theology is vital to know, to be able to look back on the exaltation of Jesus and see, because—get this—that very power is "toward us who believe, according to the working of his great might." The power that did that to Jesus is being deployed by God for the sake of you and me, his people. Isn't that extraordinary?

For any of us, life can be very hard. I know people whose marriages have been the cause or occasion of agony, just as I know people whose singleness has been the same. Even during the course of writing this chapter I have had a recurrence of these periods of anxiety. What I've just been writing from Ephesians, I am not writing just for you; I'm writing for myself as well. I need to be reminded of this power God is using for me. I need to know that while there is so much beyond my capacity to handle, there is nothing beyond his. I don't need to worry about facing more than I can cope with; I only need to worry about facing more than God can cope with. And that thought gives me good cheer.

Conclusion

Since I started writing this book, a great friend has gotten engaged; another, a job in a different country; and I've been living in the United States on a five-month placement of sorts. So, as we say where I come from, things are a little topsy-turvy. Life doesn't tend to stay still. I've learned how to drive on the other side of the road. I've had to switch the spell-check on my laptop to US English, which feels like some sort of betrayal of my country. But on the other hand, I have been a loyal ambassador of Marmite, a British savory spread that looks to most Americans like something you hose off stricken seabirds whenever there has been an oil spill. To be fair, it pretty much tastes like that too.

I have no idea what the next year is going to look like. Part of me feels that the Lord is prompting me to move, the thought of which absolutely terrifies me. But then sometimes the thought of not moving terrifies me more, if God would have me stay where I am. I really don't know. I pray for guidance and for God to be unsubtle.

That God doesn't change is more and more of a comfort. It's not to say that he's static. He is always on the move. But he is a constant. He never shifts the goalposts or abruptly rethinks the way he's been doing everything. He doesn't go through phases. He's not faddish. He surprises but only in the sense of shocking us with ever-deeper realizations of who he has always been and how he has always worked. That an unchanging God manages to somehow keep surprising us probably says far more about us than about him. He is counterintuitive.

Our response to a God like this is not to fret. It is not to wish him to be more like us, more aligned with our ways of thinking and acting. Instead we need to conform ourselves to him. He's so much smarter than we are.

I'm glad to belong to a church that regularly uses the Lord's Prayer in corporate worship. It gets to the heart of what makes following Jesus so different from any other belief system. It cuts across all our instincts:

> Our Father in heaven,
> hallowed be your name.
> Your kingdom come,
> your will be done,
>   on earth as it is in heaven.
> Give us this day our daily bread,
> and forgive us our debts,
>   as we also have forgiven our debtors.
> And lead us not into temptation,
>   but deliver us from evil.
> For yours is the kingdom, the power, and the glory forever
>   and ever. Amen. (See Matt. 6:9–13)

When Jesus teaches us to pray, he doesn't seek to bend God to our ways, but to bend ourselves to his. We pray for his name, his kingdom, and his will. Not only are we to pray for these, but as we do so, we find ourselves increasingly longing for them. I know that the elevation of my name, the implementation of my agenda, the growth of my power—these won't bless me or anyone else. The world will not be a better place if it is being conformed to my vision for it. On my better days, I am sufficiently aware of that to pray the way Jesus instructs us to. *Lord, please don't give me what I want; give me what you want.*

When I started this project, my initial aim was to write about the goodness of singleness. It is often maligned or demeaned in the church today. I wanted to redress that. I still do, and I hope this book will help. But through it all I have been increasingly preoccupied with something else—not the goodness of singleness but the goodness of God. The issue is not whether this path or that path is better, whether singleness or marriage would bring me more good. The issue is God and whether I will plunge myself into him, trusting him every day.

David famously reminds us, "Surely goodness and mercy shall follow me / all the days of my life" (Ps. 23:6). A more literal translation of "follow" is "pursue." We're not going to be able to get away from God's goodness and mercy. They're like a spiritual motorcade that will always accompany us. The more we grasp this, the less either marriage or singleness should ultimately matter to us. Let's aim for more of God, assured that whatever happens, we will never outpace his kindness to us.

Appendix

Four Ways to Avoid Sexual Sin

Life has a grain to it. Like paper and wood, it has its own inbuilt directionality. The universe is fashioned in such a way that it has an underlying structure. It follows a certain pattern with certain contours. In order to live well we need to live in a way that runs with this grain and not against it. This is where the book of Proverbs comes in.

Proverbs 5 is all about how committing sexual sin goes against the grain of how we're made. The primary target audience is the young married man, and the passage warns him against the adulteress. You may not be young or married or a man. But the wisdom of this text applies to you as much as to anyone else. Committing adultery with a woman is not the only form of sexual sin, but it follows a pattern that is common to all. Listening to this passage helps all of us.

As the passage unfolds, it presents to us four steps we need to take to avoid sexual sin.

1. Flee from Temptation

The author begins with an exhortation to listen:

> My son, be attentive to my wisdom;
>> incline your ear to my understanding. (v. 1)

The fact is, there are different kinds of listening. There's the idle listening when you're forty years old, and a member of the airline cabin crew is explaining how to fasten a seat belt. You can manage to be doing any number of other things at the same time without losing any crucial information. And then there's the very different kind of listening when the doctor is explaining to you how a medication could well save your life. You hang off every word and don't miss a single syllable. Proverbs is talking about this second kind of listening. Pay attention. Listen well. This could save your life.

In fact, listen well to this, and you will become the kind of person that others ought to listen to:

> that you may keep discretion,
> > and your lips may guard knowledge. (v. 2)

So what's the big deal? Well, lips can preserve knowledge, and they can also drip honey. Enter the adulteress:

> For the lips of a forbidden woman drip honey,
> > and her speech is smoother than oil. (v. 3)

Notice the writer just assumes we will face this kind of temptation. It is assumed that there will be a sweetness and a smoothness to the lure of sexual sin. It sounds good. We sense it will taste good. Being tempted in this way is an indication not that we have failed as Christians but that we are normal ones. If we were somehow immune, this verse wouldn't need to be in the Bible. But here it is, and the writer assumes that we, the readers, need it. Badly need it. If you are reading this passage, you are the kind of person who needs to know how sexual sin works so that you can be prepared to fight it.

So lesson one is this: sexual sin is attractive. Let's not deny that. It has a texture and flavor that appeal to broken and distorted hearts like ours.

This is true of all temptation. No temptation is presented to us as something horrible: "Hey, here's a truly abhorrent sin for you to get your teeth into. It'll completely devastate your life and leave you feeling disgusting for the rest of your life. You want in?" No, sin is much more alluring. It feels natural, like it will meet a deep need, like it's on your side. This is perhaps especially true of sexual temptation.

Proverbs 5 certainly assumes it is true both of the temptation and of the person we're feeling tempted by. There are certain kinds of people with whom the Bible forbids us to have sexual intimacy. They're married, or you are. They're not a believer, and you are. Or they're the same gender as you. The Bible is clear on these things. But when we are in the heat of temptation, it feels very different. The temptation seems so lovely, and this kind of intimacy feels so right. Nothing feels particularly wrong about it. The sin is dripping with honey and speaking with silky smoothness. But the promise could not be more different from what, in fact, results.

Sexual sin is attractive. We do ourselves no favors if we pretend otherwise. We need to acknowledge that such sin is not beneath us.

Sexual sin is also addictive. Look at how all this ends:

> The iniquities of the wicked ensnare him,
>   and he is held fast in the cords of his sin. (v. 22)

We tend to think that sexual sin is a means of relieving tension. We're wrestling with temptation, and this is just a way to get it all out of our system. We think we'll then be able to move on and get back to where things should be. We've paid our dues, so the temptation will go away.

But it doesn't. The opposite actually happens. These are deeds that ensnare and bind us. Each time we give in to sexual sin, we are giving it more control over us. We are training ourselves to find sexual fulfillment in this particular way. We are giving ourselves to it. Like any appetite, the more we feed it, the more it grows. Over time it will take more and more for it to be satisfied. The more we do it, the more we will feel the need to do it, the easier it will be to do it, and the harder it will become to stop. It will have increasing power over us. With each step, we tighten its grip on our lives.

So the point is simple. We need to flee:

> And now, O sons, listen to me,
>> and do not depart from the words of my mouth.
> Keep your way far from her,
>> and do not go near the door of her house. (vv. 7–8)

It is easy to think that we're the kind of person who can get close to this sin and then stop before it's too late. We think to ourselves that it'll be fine to start down this road and then just turn back when we've gone far enough. We expect to be able to negotiate with it. Biblical wisdom says the opposite. Run, don't walk, away from this. Don't go near it. Don't even look at it.

It is something of an understatement to say that I am not a good runner. On the very rare occasions I'll decide to go for a run, applying the word *run* to what I do is somewhat generous. It is essentially walking with a slight bounce. People with walking frames are able to overtake me. People standing still have a good chance of overtaking me.

A few years ago I was walking home late one night and decided to save time by taking a shortcut through a short alleyway. You know that in any story, the moment an alleyway is mentioned, it's not good news. Well, I discovered there were three or four guys in the alleyway. I decided to walk past them and to look entirely at ease. But just as I passed, one of them jumped out at me. I have no idea if he intended to rob or attack me or just wanted to terrify me. I didn't stay around long enough to find out. My feet barely touched the ground on the final half-mile home. I discovered that night that I can run pretty fast.

So the question is, which of these two kinds of running characterizes our flight from sexual sin? Is it token, almost leisurely? Or is it life-and-death urgent? Fleeing sexual sin means deliberately keeping as great a distance from it as we can. It means doing all we can to avoid it. For some of us, that means restricting what we look at online, or not watching certain TV shows, or being more careful about the social situations we attend, or maybe breaking up with someone, even if that person means the world to us, or maybe even changing our job. The question is not what seems to be enough to avoid sin but what is the most we can do. Proverbs says it is worth taking a long detour to ensure we don't go near it.

If any of this seems like an overreaction, listen again to how it all ends:

> He dies for lack of discipline,
> and because of his great folly he is led astray. (v. 23)

Sexual sin is attractive and addictive, a lethal combination. It'll send us into the tall grass and even into the grave. Any action and sacrifice are worth avoiding that.

2. Consider the Future

We've been shown something of why sexual sin is so tempting. Now we are shown more of where it all eventually leads. The writer wants us to see what it all comes to in the end:

> At the end of your life you groan,
> when your flesh and body are consumed. (v. 11)

Sexual sin has consequences. However much we talk about it as a "fling" or "one-night stand," the fact is that sexual sins are not so easily containable. We can find ourselves having to live with the consequences for the rest of our lives. We see what some of these are. So listen to what would be your future self if you chose to go down this path. And notice the dominant note of regret:

> Do not go near the door of her house,
> lest you give your honor to others
> > and your years to the merciless,
> lest strangers take their fill of your strength,
> > and your labors go to the house of a foreigner. (vv. 8–10)

Sexual sin costs you your strength. Your energy and vitality go into having to cope with the fallout. It could be anything from acrimony to blackmail, from lawsuits to child support. Your resources—economic, physical, emotional—are all spent on this. It can take many years from you.

The warning continues:

> And at the end of your life you groan,
> > when your flesh and body are consumed,
> and you say, "How I hated discipline,
> > and my heart despised reproof!
> I did not listen to the voice of my teachers
> > or incline my ear to my instructors.
> I am at the brink of utter ruin
> > in the assembled congregation. (vv. 11–14)

Sexual sin seems so attractive now, but fast-forward to the very end, and it all looks different.

The fact is, experience is not the best way to learn. Not when it comes to this. I've heard a number of parents say something to the effect that when it comes to their kids and this issue, it's better for them to learn from their own mistakes. A bit of boundary breaking here and heartache there, and they'll pick up some important life lessons. It's all part of growing up. Let them get on with it with no parental interference.

It's funny, but I've yet to meet a parent who takes a similar approach to their kids' learning to drive. "I'm not going to tell them what to do. Let them wrap the car around a few trees and then they'll figure it all out." We know that the consequences of mistakes behind the wheel are potentially too serious to risk our kids making them. But the consequences of mistakes made in the bedroom can be just as serious.

So listen to your potential future self. Sexual sin looks good now. But it could cost everything. Your joy, your strength. It could sap the very life out of you. What we do now can either bless us or haunt us for the rest of our lives. I know that, right now, it doesn't seem that way, but it does. It will. I know people who are a complete mess in their forties and fifties because of how they spent their twenties and thirties. So be kind to your future self. Listen to what this man says:

> You say, "How I hated discipline,
> and my heart despised reproof!
> I did not listen to the voice of my teachers
> or incline my ear to my instructors." (vv. 12–13)

Don't be too proud to listen to wisdom. Don't assume you know what you need to know about all this. Don't think your instincts are sufficiently developed. However much you might have some of this figured out, the sheer tonnage of what you still need to learn is more than you could even imagine.

3. Uphold Your Marriage

So far we have been given negative reasons for avoiding sexual sin. But for the young man tempted to commit adultery, the writer has something positive to say as well. He needs to see that it's overwhelmingly positive to uphold his marriage. And so the passage counsels him to enjoy sexual fulfillment within it:

> Drink water from your own cistern,
>> flowing water from your own well.
> Should your springs be scattered abroad,
>> streams of water in the streets?
> Let them be for yourself alone,
>> and not for strangers with you.
> Let your fountain be blessed,
>> and rejoice in the wife of your youth,
>> a lovely deer, a graceful doe.
> Let her breasts fill you at all times with delight;
>> be intoxicated always in her love. (vv. 15–19)

I remember when I started reading the Bible for the first time. We were a group of teenagers who'd meet together to talk about our reading and what we thought about it. Although we were all pretty new to reading and discussing Scripture, it really didn't take us long to discover this reference to breasts in Proverbs 5. We thought it was hilarious that the Bible mentioned breasts. But this just goes to show that our Christianity was more prudish than the Bible's. The Bible is not at all embarrassed by the enjoyment of sex in marriage. In fact, the teenage me didn't know the half of it. Some of the imagery here leaves little to the imagination:

> Drink water from your own cistern,
>> flowing water from your own well. (v. 15)

> Let your fountain be blessed,
>> and rejoice in the wife of your youth. (v. 18)

"Cistern" and "well" are both images of female sexuality, as the fountain is of male sexuality. We shouldn't be surprised to see such imagery in the Bible. After all, God is the one who invented sex. He was the one who designed human sexuality and enabled the husband and wife to enjoy their sexual union. It is to be rejoiced in and celebrated. He didn't give us a purely functional means of procreation, but one that is meant to be deeply pleasurable. It is, we could say, to be expected. God is triune, eternally Father, Son, and Holy Spirit. We know these three persons of the Trinity delight in their deep union with one another, and this love then overflows into the creation of new life. Perhaps it is no surprise that he has created us with a capacity for such a deep and joyful union that is also the means of bringing new life into the world.

It is important to remember that delight in sex is meant to be entirely mutual. This passage is addressed to a man, so it is spoken from his perspective. But it is equally true of the way in which the wife is to be delighted and intoxicated by the sexual love of her husband. Paul makes this clear in the New Testament:

> The husband should give to his wife her conjugal rights, and likewise the wife to her husband. For the wife does not have authority over her own body, but the husband does. Likewise the husband does not have authority over his own body, but the wife does. (1 Cor. 7:3–4)

Both the wife and the husband are to uphold their marriage by delighting in their sexual union. So the writer concludes:

> Why should you be intoxicated, my son, with a forbidden
> woman
> and embrace the bosom of an adulteress? (v. 20)

I love the realism of the Bible. There is alternative intoxication on offer. Again, he's not telling us to avoid adultery because it won't be in any way pleasurable. The truth is the opposite. It can feel every bit as heady and dizzying as romantic fulfillment within marriage. But we know how devastating the fallout of adultery can be. It can wreck a whole life, emotionally, physically, spiritually, and economically. The New Testament sums it up in remarkable economy as "the fleeting pleasures of sin" (Heb. 11:25). There is pleasure. It won't help us to resist temptation by pretending otherwise. But it is only fleeting. Some moments of intoxication, yes. But ruin afterward.

So, married friends, uphold your marriage. Work at your sex life. Some of us who are not married can't imagine ever needing to be told that, but the sad reality is that a healthy sex life in marriage is far from automatic. I've had even young couples share with me that they've not had sex in many months, in some cases years. Older couples regularly have to contend with changes in libido and the affects of aging on sexuality, and they need to be able to talk about these things. And, it probably goes without saying, investment in a healthy sex life is not likely to happen without investment in the marriage relationship as a whole, building and deepening the friendship that lies at the heart of it.

But what about those of us who are single? This kind of language can be painful. It's hard to hear of the intoxication of sexual satisfaction. This is something many of us long for but have never had, or previously had and now fear we will never have again.

But we too need to heed this teaching in Proverbs. We need to pray for the marriages around us, for their protection and flourishing. We have a stake in their being strong. It may mean asking married friends how we can support them as a wife or a husband. We need to uphold the Bible's teaching in our own lives, honoring the marriage bed by living lives of purity. And we need to uphold the marriage we have in Christ. The language of intoxication that can be so hard to hear is a picture of what we will experience in eternity with Christ. We are pledged to him and need to honor our relationship with him by remaining faithful to him.

4. Remember That God Is Watching

All we do and say and think takes place in the full view of God:

> For a man's ways are before the eyes of the LORD,
>   and he ponders all his paths. (Prov. 5:21)

The eyes of God miss nothing in all we do. And lest we think he has a somewhat glazed look when it comes to what we do, the second part of Proverbs 5:21 reminds us that all God sees, he takes in and ponders. All our paths he reflects on and weighs in his mind.

This is a warning to us.

Some of us are good at getting away with all sorts of things. Even in such a connected world, it is possible to lead a double life. Affairs can be concealed and addictions carried out entirely in private. We may be adept at looking at all sorts of material on our devices that no one else knows anything about. There will be some reading this who have no idea that their spouse is being unfaithful or that their child is viewing horrific porn on their phone.

But nothing will escape the scrutiny of God. It just isn't possible.

A while ago, one of the major highways near my hometown was undergoing roadwork as they added a couple of new lanes and resurfaced others. It meant that for well over a year, only about half the lanes were available for us while all the construction went on. As well as the increased congestion, this also meant a greatly reduced speed limit, which also meant the placement of speed cameras to track everyone's speed. This was the first time many of us had encountered these. A friend whose commute took him on this road every day discovered some ways to evade the cameras. He knew where each camera was and managed to sneak behind a huge truck at exactly the right time to avoid being seen. Unchecked by the cameras, he could then drive as fast as he wanted.

That may work with a speed camera. It doesn't work with God. We may be able to deceive other people; we will never deceive God. There is simply no thought he hasn't seen and doesn't know everything about. He knows every webpage we've viewed and every fantasy that has drifted across our mind. The very secrets of our heart are entirely open to him. Things we don't even know about our motives and lusts, he understands fully. He misses nothing. He is impossible to fool. The book of Hebrews reminds us:

> No creature is hidden from his sight, but all are naked and exposed to the eyes of him to whom we must give account. (Heb. 4:13)

There is no ultimate security in incognito web browsing. God sees every word we type into our search engines. God sees. God ponders. And one day we will give an account to him for each and every thing we have thought and done.

But there is also encouragement in these verses. God sees our sin. He also sees every striving to be pure and godly. He knows when we are battling; he knows what we are going through.

There are times when we are assaulted by sexual temptation, and it can be distressing. We are devastated by some of the inclinations of our own hearts. We long for our desires to be pure and godly rather than disordered and base. We flee and we fight but are left discouraged and weary. God sees all this too. And more than that, as Hebrews goes on to remind us:

> Since then we have a great high priest who has passed through the heavens, Jesus, the Son of God, let us hold fast our confession. For we do not have a high priest who is unable to sympathize with our weaknesses, but one who in every respect has been tempted as we are, yet without sin. (Heb. 4:14–15)

We all struggle in a variety of ways. It may well be that no one really seems to understand the kind of struggle you face or knows the pain you go through as you fight temptation. But Jesus does. He suffered with us. And he suffered for us. That makes him a great Savior to pray to. As we collect wounds from the battles of life in this world and come to him desperate for his help and protection, he does not roll his eyes. When we come in heartfelt repentance for the times when we have failed, he does not step back with his arms folded. He draws near to us as we draw near to him. As we strive to be faithful to him, often in the midst of an unsympathetic and scornful world, he sees us. Our labors for him are never unnoticed.

Notes

Introduction

1. See John Lloyd and David Mitchinson, *The QI Book of General Ignorance* (Faber & Faber, 2006).
2. See Albert Y. Hsu, *The Single Issue* (London: Inter-Varsity Press, 1998), 9.
3. Quoted in Kate Wharton, *Single-Minded: Being Single, Whole and Living Life to the Full* (Oxford, UK: Monarch, 2013), 29.

Chapter 1: Singleness Is Too Hard

1. I am grateful to my friend Ed Shaw for pointing these out. See his *Same-Sex Attraction and the Church: The Surprising Plausibility of the Celibate Life* (Downers Grove, IL: InterVarsity Press, 2015), 105.
2. For more detailed discussion on this, see D. A. Carson, *Matthew 13–28*, Expositor's Bible Commentary (Grand Rapids, MI: Zondervan, 1995), 419.
3. See Barry Danylak, *Redeeming Singleness: How the Storyline of Scripture Affirms the Single Life* (Wheaton, IL: Crossway, 2010), 153.
4. Ibid., 157.
5. Vaughan Roberts, *True Spirituality: The Challenge of 1 Corinthians for the Twenty-First-Century Church* (Nottingham, UK: Inter-Varsity Press, 2011), 101.

Chapter 2: Singleness Requires a Special Calling

1. Mike Cosper, *The Stories We Tell: How TV and Movies Long for and Echo the Truth* (Wheaton, IL: Crossway, 2014). An excellent book, by the way.
2. Albert Y. Hsu, *The Single Issue* (London: Inter-Varsity Press, 1998), 55.
3. Ibid.
4. Timothy Keller, *The Meaning of Marriage* (New York: Dutton, 2011), 207–8.

5. Ibid.

6. Vaughan Roberts, *True Spirituality: The Challenge of 1 Corinthians for the Twenty-First-Century Church* (Nottingham, UK: Inter-Varsity Press, 2011), 88.

7. Paul Barnett, *1 Corinthians: Holiness and Hope of a Rescued People*, Focus on the Bible (Ross-shire, UK: Christian Focus: 2000), 112.

8. Roberts, *True Spirituality*, 90.

9. John MacArthur, "Children in the Shade," lecture, Council for Biblical Manhood and Womanhood National Conference, April 2016, accessed August 2017, https://www.youtube.com/watch?v=D7S_zeOxd-g.

10. Keller, *The Meaning of Marriage*, 201–2.

11. See Ben Sasse, *The Vanishing American Adult: Our Coming-of-Age Crisis and How to Rebuild a Culture of Self-Reliance* (New York: St. Martin's Press, 2017).

Chapter 3: Singleness Means No Intimacy

1. C. S. Lewis, *The Four Loves* (1960; repr. New York: HarperCollins, 2002), 73.

2. Ed Shaw, *Same-Sex Attraction and the Church: The Surprising Plausibility of the Celibate Life* (Downers Grove, IL: IVP Books, 2015), 71.

3. Ibid., 72.

4. Lewis, *Four Loves*, 70.

5. Wesley Hill, *Spiritual Friendship: Finding Love in the Church as a Celibate Gay Christian* (Grand Rapids, MI: Brazos Press, 2015), 8.

6. Lewis, *Four Loves*, 70.

7. Raymond C. Ortlund Jr., *Proverbs*, Preaching the Word (Wheaton, IL: Crossway, 2012), 166.

8. Lewis, *Four Loves*, 74.

9. Derek Kidner, *Proverbs*, Tyndale Old Testament Commentaries, ed. Donald J. Wiseman (1968; repr. Downers Grove, IL: IVP Academic, 2008), 158.

Chapter 4: Singleness Means No Family

1. If you're particularly observant, you may have realized that Jesus doesn't promise "fathers" in this verse. This is most probably a reflection of what Jesus says elsewhere about fathers—"Call no man your father on earth, for you have one Father, who is in heaven" (Matt. 23:9). This will be easily misunderstood if not read alongside other comments Jesus makes. Elsewhere he reinforces the Old Testament command to "honor your father and your mother" (Ex. 20:12)

and rebukes those who fail to (see Mark 7:9–13). Jesus is therefore not asking us to deny our earthly fathers—we are still obligated to them—but is using hyperbole to show how the fatherhood of God eclipses all others.

2. Ed Shaw, *Same-Sex Attraction and the Church: The Surprising Plausibility of the Celibate Life* (Downers Grove, IL: IVP Books, 2015), 42.

3. Andrea Trevenna, *The Heart Of Singleness: How to be Single and Satisfied* (Purcellville, VA: Good Book Co., 2013), 90.

4. Rosaria Butterfield, *The Gospel Comes with a House Key* (Wheaton, IL: Crossway, 2018).

5. Raymond C. Ortlund Jr., *Proverbs*, Preaching the Word (Wheaton, IL: Crossway, 2012), 168.

6. John Piper, *This Momentary Marriage: A Parable of Permanence* (Wheaton, IL: Crossway, 2009), 109.

7. Ibid., 110.

8. Barry Danylak, *Redeeming Singleness: How the Storyline of Scripture Affirms the Single Life* (Wheaton, IL: Crossway: 2010), 141.

9. Piper, *This Momentary Marriage*, 111.

10. C. S. Lewis, *The Great Divorce* (1946; repr. London: HarperCollins, 2002), 119. Bethany Jenkins references the same section in "Turning 40 While Single and Childless," The Gospel Coalition website, October 5, 2016, accessed July 8, 2017, https://www.thegospelcoalition.org/article/turning-40-while-single-and-childless.

11. Jenkins, "Turning 40 While Single and Childless."

12. Matthew Anderson (@mattleeanderson), Twitter, April 28, 2017.

Chapter 5: Singleness Hinders Ministry

1. Albert Mohler, "Must a Pastor Be Married? *The New York Times* Asks the Question," AlbertMohler.com, accessed July 3, 2017, http://www.albertmohler.com/2011/03/25/must-a-pastor-be-married-the-new-york-times-asks-the-question/.

2. Quoted in Erik Eckholm, "Unmarried Pastor, Seeking a Job, Sees Bias," *New York Times* website, March 21, 2011, accessed July 3, 2017, http://www.nytimes.com/2011/03/22/us/22pastor.html?_r=2.

3. Barry Danylak, *Redeeming Singleness: How the Storyline of Scripture Affirms the Single Life* (Wheaton, IL: Crossway, 2010), 158.

4. Ibid.; emphasis original.

Chapter 6: Singleness Wastes Your Sexuality

1. "N. T. Wright on Gay Marriage," *First Things*, https://www.firstthings.com/blogs/firstthoughts/2014/06/n-t-wrights-argument-against-same-sex-marriage, accessed June 30, 2018.

2. N. T. Wright, "From Genesis to Revelation: An Anglican Perspective," in *Not Just Good, but Beautiful: The Complementary Relationship between Man and Woman*, ed. Helen Alvaré and Steven Lopes (Walden, NY: Plough, 2015), 87.

3. I am grateful to Ray Ortlund for drawing this surprise to my attention.

4. Raymond C. Ortlund Jr., *Marriage and the Mystery of the Gospel* (Wheaton, IL: Crossway, 2016), 19.

5. Wright, "From Genesis to Revelation," 88.

6. Raymond C. Ortlund Jr., *Proverbs*, Preaching the Word (Wheaton, IL: Crossway, 2012), 16.

7. Ibid., 100.

8. Wright, "From Genesis to Revelation," 96.

9. "The Form of Solemnization of Marriage," in the Book of Common Prayer.

10. Glynn Harrison, *A Better Story: God, Sex, and Human Flourishing* (London: Inter-Varsity Press, 2016), 136–7.

11. Ibid., 153.

12. Ibid., 137.

Chapter 7: Singleness Is Easy

1. C. S. Lewis, *The Four Loves* (1960; repr. New York: HarperCollins, 2002), 78.

2. Kate Wharton, *Single-Minded: Being Single, Whole and Living Life to the Full* (Oxford, UK: Monarch, 2013), 21.

3. Ed Shaw, *Same-Sex Attraction and the Church: The Surprising Plausibility of the Celibate Life* (Downers Grove, IL: InterVarsity Press, 2015), 61.

4. Carrie English, "A Bridesmaid's Lament: Doesn't Friendship Deserve Some Fanfare, Too?," *Boston Globe* website, June 12, 2011, accessed June 6, 2018, http://archive.boston.com/lifestyle/weddings/articles/2011/06/12/a_bridesmaids_lament/.

5. Kathy Keller, personal email, August 8, 2017.

6. C. S. Lewis, letter to Mary Willis Shelburne, in *The Collected Letters of C. S. Lewis*, 3 vols. (New York: Harper Collins, 2007), 3:776. I am grateful to Betsy Howard for pointing out this quotation.

7. Andrea Trevenna, *The Heart Of Singleness: How to be Single and Satisfied* (Purcellville, VA: Good Book Co., 2013), 48.

General Index

Scripture Index